MY WAY:
BUILDING A SATISFYING CAREER IN SELLING

MY WAY:
BUILDING A SATISFYING CAREER IN SELLING

by

Don Van Der Weide, CLU

FARNSWORTH PUBLISHING COMPANY, INC.
Rockville Centre, New York 11570

Published by Farnsworth Publishing Co., Inc.
Rockville Centre, New York 11570.
Library of Congress Catalog Card No. 80-70927.
ISBN 0-87863-0589.
Manufactured in the United States of America.

PREFACE

THIS BOOK IS FOR YOU

There has been so much written about life insurance selling—good, solid, practical material—that one may wonder, why another book?

Perhaps it's the missionary spirit many of us possess, a zeal to share our ideas and techniques. How many life underwriter meetings or company conventions have you attended and heard sales people tell how they do it? After such meetings, how many times have you seen crowds of agents around a speaker who unselfishly gives his or her time, energy, and ideas? If you've been in the business for any period of time, you know that this is a sharing business. We share, not only with the agents in our own company, but with the agents in all companies.

That's why I wrote this book—because I feel I have an obligation to my brothers and sisters who sell life insurance, as well as an obligation to repay those who have gone before, paving the way and making insurance one of the most highly respected products purchased by the consuming public.

As you'll see, the following pages aren't composed of gimmicky sales ideas or "up-to-the-minute" tax dodges. This is a book about an Iowa farm boy who made—and still makes—a pretty good living selling life insurance. It's a collection of my thoughts, attitudes, and approaches to the business of selling life insurance. It's time-tested material, proven over the years. If a reader secures two or three ideas which he or she can use, I'll feel that the book will have served its purpose.

If you're successful in selling life insurance, you may find the book to be interesting and valuable, comparing your operation with mine. As you review my business methods and philosophies, you may find something which you can apply to your operation. My system has been working successfully for over 20 years. It works for me, and some of it, undoubtedly, will work for you.

If you've been in the life insurance business for a number of years and have not achieved the success you wanted, you may find some useful items in this book. With many people, the difference between making a living and making a *good* living is simply putting more emphasis on certain key factors. You'll find these ingredients in this book.

If you're relatively new to selling life insurance, I think you'll discover a lot of practical material. I attribute much of my success to plain hard work and following the rules which have been developed by hundreds of thousands of life insurance agents over the past 100 years. I believe you'll be helped by specific chapters and by specific guidance on such things as setting goals, attitudes, and getting out of slumps.

Too many times we gaze from a distance at those who really seem to be making it in this business. The distance lends enchantment, and they appear to be superstars. Yet every one of them had their early years in the business, had their doubts, and had their share of failure. And many of them are still shaky when calling on new prospects and still have their fear of failure. They're human beings with all the attendant natural failings.

This book tells how I did it, and how I'm still doing it. And anything *I* can do, *you* can do if you want to. I sincerely believe that. So, read on. I suggest you read straight through the book the first time to get the general feel of it. Then pick out chapters which have special meaning to you and study the practical items you may wish to adopt. Keep the book near at hand and, as time permits, review the material which has special interest for you.

As I said, this business has been good to me, and I hope it will be good to you. There is no other business which pays off for intelligent hard work as well as life insurance selling. My career is proof of that, and yours can be, too.

CONTENTS

INTRODUCTION

For 23 years Don Van Der Weide has sold life insurance within a 50-mile radius of his hometown, Orange City, Iowa, population just 4,000. The year he became President of the New York Life Top Club—the designation awarded to our Company's leading agent in terms of first-year commissions—he was responsible for placing $31 million of life business on our books. It can hardly be said that Don had one lucky year; the two years before his designation as Top Club President, he was runner-up in the competition involving approximately 10,000 agents across the United States and Canada.

How did he do it? "My Way: Building A Satisfying Career In Selling" gives some clear and precise answers to this question. Ever-increasing production goals, personal and office organization, self discipline, and hard work are all part of it. So is professionalism, which Don defines as placing the interests of one's prospect or client first at all times, and keeping up with product design changes, tax developments, and clients' personal situations. In this book, Don emphasizes the importance of the simple presentation and the need to organize the office so that the agent can concentrate on what he or she does best: selling insurance.

Eunice Van Der Weide, Don's wife and partner in every sense, writes her own chapter about her husband's "Journey." She describes how she compiles lists of prospects, attends Company conventions, monitors trends in the industry and acts as Don's sounding board. They have found considerable satisfaction in being able to work together in a way that few couples find possible today.

Don mentions, in his final paragraph, that the book was fun to write. I would add that it was both fun and illuminating to read. It is an American success story based on industry and intelligence; Don places absolutely no reliance on gimmicks or secret sales methods. All of us in the life insurance industry can take pride in Don's career, which is a role model for other agents seeking to improve not only the quantity of their production, but the quality of their service to clients.

Finally, I must add a word about my personal appreciation in being asked to write this introduction. Don and I have been friends and business associates for many years, and I have had the pleasure of seeing him develop into the successful insurance professional that he has become. He has also been most generous with his time in helping us make corporate plans and decisions. I am grateful for this opportunity to acknowledge publicly the high regard in which all of us at New York Life hold Don Van Der Weide.

R. Manning Brown, Jr.
Chairman of the Board
New York Life Insurance Company
March, 1981

1.

THE END OF THE RACE

The evening of June 30, 1978 was a warm one in Iowa. As I sat in the den of my home in Orange City, I could almost hear the corn growing in the fields outside of town, meeting a deadline to be "high as an elephant's eye by the fourth of July." But my mind wasn't on corn. It was on a race I had just run, a race in which the winner would be the president of my company's Top Club. If I seemed particularly tired tonight, I mused, it must be because this was the fourth time I had run the race. And it would be days before I knew if I had won.

We measure growth by looking back at where we were and comparing it to where we are. That night, I had ample time to look back. There was nothing more that I could do physically. The race was over. It was now time for the computers in the Home Office to calculate the final results, to determine which agent had earned the most in first-year commissions—the yardstick for the presidency.

I went into the kitchen and fixed myself a glass of iced tea. The house was quiet except for the soft sound of the stereo which my wife, Eunice, had turned on. As my partner for almost a quarter-century, she knew what thoughts were in my mind and how I needed some time to just sit and think. And think I did.

My thoughts went back 21 years to 1957—the day I entered the life insurance business. I was 24 years old. I had graduated from Morningside College and had finished a two-year hitch in the United States Army. Eunice and I had been married for about two years, and we had a two-month old daughter, Debbie. I was looking for a career, and teaching school seemed like a good idea to me. I like people and enjoy working with them. In addition, I had gone through college on a basketball scholarship. Teaching and coaching seemed like a good deal.

I had attached some other specifications to my life's career. It would have to be emotionally and financially rewarding. And it would have to be in or near Orange City, Iowa. I was born there, grew up there, and wanted to spend the rest of my life in Orange City.

I smiled as I recalled the mental gymnastics that I went through in choosing between a teaching career and a career of selling life insurance. Teaching would be rewarding and could eventually lead to the position of school superintendent—with an annual salary of $30,000. Also, as a teacher and, possibly, a coach, I could fit in some part-time selling of life insurance to supplement my income.

In considering life insurance sales, I realized that I could work with an even greater number of people and help them to own life insurance, a product in which I firmly believed. The decision took time to make, and it was a team decision made by both Eunice and me. I signed my sales contract on August 1, 1957.

So that you will have a good idea of the market in which I found myself selling, let me tell you a little bit about Orange City. Orange City, I admit with some bias, is a beautiful town which reflects its Dutch heritage. There are ornamental windmills, a factory that makes wooden shoes, and an annual tulip festival. Parking is never a problem. The air is fresh; the streets are clean; nearly everybody has the midday meal at home. The horizon around Orange City is a sultry sea of soybeans and cornstalks, with much of the corn being used to fatten the livestock, primarily steers, on the same farms.

The population of the town is 4,000. Not many people to support a life insurance agent, you say? Yet for 23 years I have sold life insurance within a 50-mile radius of Orange City. About one-third of the people who live in town are my clients, and I have a total of 3,000 clients. In this market, I've sold from *200 to 400 policies each year.* I started selling people with whom I did business, people who belonged to my church, and people who belonged to the same organizations that I did.

Guideline for Success

My first manager gave me a beautifully simple idea which has been one of my guidelines for success over the past 23 years. I recommend it to you enthusiastically. He gave me a ledger book (which I still use). *He said that if I filled a page of that book each month with the names of applicants, my income would take care of itself.*

At first, I tried for 10 applicants a month. In those early days, I sold many family plans, and I invariably placed term riders on whatever permanent coverage I sold. I became dissatisfied with only 10 apps because I found myself with too much idle time. So I tried for 15, then 20, and then 25. As you can see, I believe in numbers. *The agent who writes many cases cannot help but be successful.* Case rate truly is the name of the game.

Most of the people who bought from me in my early days were about the same age I was. I made a special effort, however, to write insurance on people who were older than I was for a very simple reason: they could make intelligent buying decisions much more quickly. From the start, I became a general practitioner. I sold the entire line—life, health, annuities, group. I felt that if I didn't sell all of my company's products, I'd be shortchanging the people I served—and myself, too. (For example, one employee of a business to which I had sold group insurance could not be helped medically in the United States. So he was treated in Europe, and my company, without hesitation, paid most of the medical bill.)

Early in my career, I learned another guideline for success. From the start, I have pursued the selling of life insurance from a professional point of view. What do I mean by the term "professional"? I mean that the premium paid—or the commission earned—is of no consequence at all. *The real issue is to solve the problem being faced by the prospective policyowner.* If the policy solves the problem, the policyowner will cheerfully pay the premium. This gives me the freedom to be truly professional and to quickly and honestly get the point across to a prospect that I am really there to help. My remuneration is truly secondary.

Whenever I get in front of a new prospect, I try to see myself as that person sees me. In all my dealings with people, I constantly try to bring out the best in myself. When I develop the best in me, the best invariably comes out of everyone with whom I touch base. Right from the start, I considered all my policyowners to be friends. In the final analysis, it's really not how much money you make or how many awards you win. What really counts is the number of friends you have made. What better way to make friends than to sell life insurance?

As I poured my second glass of iced tea in the kitchen that night, I thought of the success I have enjoyed. Eunice and I built our home in Orange City, we had a second child—a son, Tim—and my insurance sales work provided us with a comfortable income. I had become a regional officer of my company's Top Club, a sign of substantial sales performance. And now I was seeking national office in the Top Club.

Membership in Top Clubs

Let me explain what this membership in Top Clubs entails. New York Life, like most insurance companies, has several "clubs" which are signs of an agent's sales performance. In our clubs, membership is attained primarily by first-year commissions. To become a member of a specific club, an agent must earn first-year commissions of a specified amount. The company is split geographically into 17 regions (including Canada). You can become "regional vice president" of your region by having the highest amount of first-year commissions of all agents in that region. The number two agent in the region is called "second vice president." The positions are honorary, of course, and, like club membership, are used to denote respective sales proficiency.

The top position in New York Life Clubs is the presidency—president of the Top Club. The number two position nationally is vice president of the Top Club. The president is the agent who has earned the most in first-year commissions (former presidents are not included in this determination since you can be president only once).

The vice president is the runner-up. You can be vice president more than once—as my story indicates.

A lot of outstanding life insurance agents have been president of my company's Top Club. I think the names of Ben Feldman and Ray Triplett, to name only two, are well-known throughout the industry. It is an honor to join a group like this—an honor and no mean feat.

About five years ago, I began seeking national office in the Top Club. Why? Why not just enjoy life, especially when your income is substantial and you're doing what you want to do, where you want to do it? Why take on the extra work so necessary to become president or even vice president? Perhaps the answers will become apparent as you read through this book. At this point, let me briefly explain that it's too easy to plateau when you make a company club, especially the highest one. It's too easy when you become a regional club officer to believe that you've done the best you can, that you've shown all that's in you. So, something inside me told me to enter the race.

In 1975, I had a good shot at the presidency, but I didn't make it. In 1976 and 1977, I was close—real close—but still only made vice president in those two years. Frustrating? Definitely. For three years, I did everything I could to meet my goal, but I hadn't met it. On the plus side, I had sold an enormous amount of life insurance—$70,000,000 in three years—and had been of tremendous service to prospects and clients. But still the presidency eluded me.

On July 1, 1977, I vowed to try again. It's easy to follow suggestions—well-meaning suggestions—from others to catch your breath and, perhaps, make a run for the presidency again at some later date. Relax, take a break, take a year off, recharge your batteries—and then try again. Good advice, yes, but I believe that *once the momentum is there, you can't let up.* I decided that if this is it, if this was to be the last lap of the race, I was going to have to work harder.

I became more persistent, more demanding, more unwilling to take no for an answer. I became stronger with a more positive attitude that life insurance is the only logical way to solve many financial problems. The feeling was more dominant in my life than ever before and I became more enthusiastic than ever. *I didn't change my method of operation; I merely expanded it.*

These were the thoughts that filled my mind that June night. I had given it my all—again. I had run hard for another 365 days. In a few days, I would know if I had won, come in second, or had merely been an also-ran. I was emotionally down, physically exhausted. There was nothing more that I could do since the books were closed. I drained the last few drops of iced tea and made my plans for tomorrow. I would go back to work doing the same as I did before—write insurance for the needs of children, young people, middle-aged people, and older people.

I would hear soon enough about my race for the presidency.

My Way

When we examine our lives, we realize that the amount of money in the bank or the prestige won in the community will not bring the satisfactions that add up to real happiness. What matters is what we have been and meant in the lives of others. One of the best ways to bring out the best in others is by developing the best in ourselves.

2.

THIS BUSINESS OF PROSPECTING

I've given quite a few talks throughout the United States to groups of life insurance agents. It's always a thrill, and I especially look forward to the question and answer sessions which follow my formal presentation. These sessions may take the form of questions from the floor, or they may be informal give-and-takes in a hotel lobby, at a coffee break, or at a poolside. One topic always comes up—prospecting. How do I do it? they ask. How do I prospect? How do I find people to sell life insurance to?

Good questions. Without prospects, you're out of business. How can you sell life insurance if you don't have any prospects? You may be the most gifted salesperson in the world, but what do you do if you have no one to whom to tell your story?

All good questions. And one more question invariably comes up (I smile when I see it coming): Don, how can you sell so much insurance in a town that has only 4,000 people?

I have answers for all these questions. Without my prospects, I would not be where I am today. I have no secret methods of prospecting. I do what most other successful agents do. When I started selling life insurance, I used methods most new agents use. As I became more successful, my methods were the same as others who had blazed the trail.

How I Started To Prospect

You'll remember that in the first chapter I said that I started selling to people with whom I did business, people who belonged to my church, and people who belonged to the same organizations that I belonged to. My wife, Eunice, compiled lists of prospects for me. With her careful eye and inquiring mind, she seemed to wring out new names from what some would consider a limited market. The local newspaper, as well as church and college newspapers, were sources she checked regularly for announcements of births, weddings, and so forth.

She'd go to a women's club meeting and jot down the names of new members. When we went out for a social evening or friendly game of golf, we would run into people who were potential prospects, and Eunice would compile the names. From the very start, ours was a team effort.

My secretary lent similar assistance. She would look through the local newspaper, the city directory, and places where people applied for new listings for telephones and for hookups to the water system. We had a steady flow of names.

Twenty-three years ago, I looked for young families with children. These were my original prospects, my prime market. I showed them how life insurance could fill the void created by the death of the breadwinner and the subsequent loss of his earned income. I looked into the business insurance market, too, and showed business prospects how life insurance could be used in such areas as fringe benefits and corporate planning for executives and other key people. I was a general practitioner, covering many bases.

Nothing new, you say? I agree. Selling is a process of securing names, qualifying them, calling on them, and asking them to buy. I've already mentioned that I was a firm believer—right from the start—in *case rate.* I sold from 200 to 400 policies a year. And this activity led me to the real reason for my prospecting and sales success. The people I sold in the early years have turned into a *treasure chest* for me. *Eighty percent of my present business comes from these people.* So I'm not seeking new clients now—I'm trying to develop business from my client base.

If I can put this philosophy into a few simple sentences, it is this: When I began to sell life insurance 23 years ago, I had to acquire clients. Now I have clients, and I must grow with them. Their needs for life insurance have grown, and I must be of service to them by pointing out these needs and showing them how life insurance can solve them.

Your Own Treasure Chest of Prospects

If you're just getting started in the life insurance business, let me restress my original point. Write large numbers of policies each and every year. Don't let up. Develop that large base of policyowners to whom you can return every year and write more insurance. If you don't follow this simple advice, you'll find yourself compelled each and every year of your career to spend time—lots of it—in finding new prospects. This time can be put to use more profitably selling insurance. If you secure no other idea from this book than the idea of a large case rate, you'll find yourself well-rewarded for the book's purchase price. Case rate pays off now and in the future.

Prospecting is not a method of examining lists of people—from architects to zoologists—and finding out which of them wants to buy insurance. Prospecting is a method of developing additional needs for life insurance among people you've already written and on whom you have a good deal of information. Prospecting is a method of determining which people need your services and how you can make your services available to them.

Developing a System

As I grew in the life insurance business, I noticed that I had, in a sense, different "levels" of prospects. Some people were growing faster than others and thus needed more of my time, especially those who asked for it. This led to my system of qualifying prospects as "A," "B," and "C" prospects.

This was a simple way of indicating to myself which prospects needed my services and the degree to which they were needed. A "C" prospect might be a young, single person who needed a life insurance policy to get started on a lifetime of financial planning. A "B" prospect might be a young family head, possibly a new father, who needed a more complex program of life insurance, with emphasis placed on settlement options and beneficiary designations. An "A" prospect might be a business owner whose business success needed insurance planning to help insure business continuation.

My clients are important to me, no matter what their "level." I am firmly committed to providing service to each one. The classification was simply a way of indicating to myself—for time control purposes—where I should devote more time at any given point. But I'm still a general practitioner—the fives and tens are just as important as the five hundreds and the millions.

In my quest for presidency of my company's Top Club, I refined the system somewhat. I devised a system of "AAA," "AA," and "A" prospects. I had to devote more time to the "AAA" prospect because of his or her demands, needs, and expectations of me. Being of service to the "AAA" prospect paid me more per hour so that I could afford to spend more time with this prospect. It was the "AAA" and "AA" prospects which led me to the fulfillment of the higher goals I had set for myself. These people had higher needs for life insurance; these needs, in turn, led to higher life insurance sales.

There's an additional benefit to working with "AAA" and "AA" prospects. They are more of a challenge to you. If you've been in the business for any amount of time, you know that after a while, some of the challenge disappears, especially as you sharpen your sales skills. It's no longer a matter of whether you'll make enough sales to earn a living. You *know* that you can do that. You know that the law of averages is working for you, that if you call on x amount of prospects, they'll lead you to y number of sales.

Your sales presentation becomes more polished, your answers to objections more skillful and confident. The challenge starts to diminish and, perhaps, a little boredom sets in. But when you call on people with big needs for life insurance, that's where the action is. It's a little different calling on a prospect to sell a mortgage protection term policy and then calling on one who has a million dollar business continuation or estate conservation problem. With the bigger need, your juices start to flow, your senses become more finely tuned—the sale becomes an exciting process, adding a whole new sense of excitement to your selling day.

Other Ways to Prospect

I prospect in a number of other ways. For example, I do a fair amount of joint work, that is, selling with another agent. Agents will come to me and ask me to work with them on a particular prospect. I'm glad to do so. I enjoy this type of work. But I have a general rule that I insist be followed.

The other agent must secure all the facts concerning the prospect so that I can put together an idea to solve the problem. I can't afford to spend the time to "cold canvass" with another agent to find prospects. I don't do it in my own operation, so I can't do it with anyone else. The other agent must find the prospect and obtain all the information necessary for me to prepare a presentation.

Centers of influence are important to me, too. The business and professional people in my community have proven to be valuable centers for me. Generally, they are long-standing clients who direct me to other business or professional people. I've done a service for them, or else they have seen the type of service I'm capable of performing. Centers of influence have produced the large policyowner base I have. Is it any wonder that I'm high on them as a prospecting source?

While on this point, let me mention a valuable observation I've made in my life: Successful people surround themselves with successful people. They can rely on their judgments. In this regard, I have "resource" people whom I can visit for a few minutes (they're busy people and so am I) and discuss a particular need, idea, or problem—and my thoughts about a solution—and how we can devise an answer for a client. Your resource people may be centers of influence as well—lawyers, accountants, bankers, trust officers. And don't discount other life insurance agents as possible resource people for yourself.

Still More Sources of Prospects

I use referred leads. I find that there are other people in the world who may enjoy having the same service I've just now given to my client. If my client is satisfied with my service, he or she will be glad to give me the names of other people who might be able to use my talents. The key to successful use of referred leads is to get as much information on the prospect as possible before the contact. Some information may be secured from the person making the referral, some may be common knowledge in the community, and some may come from other clients who also know the prospect. The more information you can secure in advance, the stronger your selling position will be.

My staff is a good source of prospects for me. After all, they're the ones who have constant contact with my clients. If a client walks into the office or calls on the telephone, my staff makes the first contact with him or her. In the conversation that follows, my staff can pick up a lot of information which can lead to sales opportunities for me. It's wise to investigate training your staff to be aware of these possibilities and to take advantage of them, passing the information along to you for evaluation and follow-up.

Office leads are another source of prospects. By office leads, I refer to the names of prospects or policyowners given to you by your company for follow-up. A lead may be a telephone inquiry from someone who wants information, or it may be a request by a policyowner (who has no active agent) for service on, say, a change of beneficiary. I take every such lead given to me and follow it up by telephone, by letter, or in person, depending on where the prospect is. I'm interested in helping those who need assistance, and I have found that such assistance can lead to additional sales.

On the subject of prospecting, let me mention one more "help" I use. Each month, I send out a number of copies of a four-page personalized newsletter, *Planned Financial Security,* which is prepared by Farnsworth Publishing Company. This newsletter discusses a number of subjects including insurance, taxes, wills, trusts, and related matters. It's a way of keeping in touch with prospects and of building prestige with newly acquired prospects. The return in terms of sales is far in excess of the cost of the newsletter.

My Way

Life insurance agents have come a long way over the years. We had to overcome a sometimes less than appealing public image. We had to learn not to think small. We had to learn the truly remarkable potential and versatility of the product we sold. But through generations of selling experience, we have accomplished all these things. Along the way, we recognized that we were business people, that we were professionals in our chosen field, not merely because we did it well but because we were highly skilled, trained, and motivated. Today we no longer think small because the size of our operations and the weight of our responsibilities are simply too great to accommodate on a small scale. We talk in terms of our personal staffs, advertising budgets, public relations, and promotional items. We haven't merely labeled ourselves business people, we have become the heads of business enterprises. And as we all know, that means a great deal more than simply selling and servicing policies.

3.

APPROACHING PROSPECTS ABOUT LIFE INSURANCE

There are two types of prospects whom I approach about life insurance. The first type is the person who has never bought life insurance from me. In most instances, I have never met the prospect. The other type of prospect is an existing client to whom I'd like to sell more life insurance.

Calling on New Prospects

I like to get referrals from my clientele. Much of my new business comes from this source. To put myself in the strongest position possible when calling on the prospect, I ask my client if he or she would mind calling the person to whom I've been referred. In many cases, the client says he or she doesn't mind at all. Then I ask the client to pick up the phone and call the prospect, indicating that I'll be getting in touch with him or her shortly. I find that my client will generally say a few nice things about me and will mention that the prospect's time won't be wasted when speaking with me. If you've done a good job for the client and he or she is happy with your technique and service, the client will frequently call the prospect for you. This is ideal.

There are some clients who may be reluctant to call someone else for you, even if they're happy with the work you've done for them. This is understandable, and I never pressure anyone to make a call for me. I simply get the name of someone who could profit by my service, and I ask my client for permission to use his or her name when I make my contact. Most of the time this doesn't present a problem.

Let's say I have secured my client's permission to use his or her name. To save time, generally, I call the prospect and simply say something like this:

"Mr. Prospect, this is Don Van Der Weide of New York Life. I have been referred to you by a client of mine, John Smith, who, I understand, is a friend of yours. John and I have been involved with some estate planning work this past year, and John is pleased and satisfied with the work that I have done for him.

"Recently, I asked him if he knew someone who might appreciate the kind of work I have done for him, and he mentioned your name. Now it is possible that you have already done everything that John has done. If so, I commend you. But if not, I would be willing to try to fit you into my schedule for the purpose of determining if I can be of some help to you. Would tomorrow morning at 9:30 be convenient for me to stop by and get acquainted and to find out if I can be of some service to you throughout the next year?"

As you can see, this is a simple, direct approach. It's the same approach used by my secretary if she calls the prospect to secure the appointment.

From time to time, I'll call in-person, and when I do, my approach goes very much like the telephone approach. I really feel that I don't want to try to be someone different than who I really am and, as a result, I feel that most of my approaches are identical. Sincerity and genuineness are very important in selling life insurance.

The decision of whether to phone or drop in on a prospect is generally made by me. At times, I feel that I would much rather have an appointment to see the individual than just drop in. This saves time and shows respect for my prospect's time, a point I stress when I call. Most of the time, my initial approach to a prospect is on the telephone.

Call Reluctance

Call reluctance is always a problem. I never feel that I'm fully equipped when I go on a call. I could be better prepared, I feel, although I've prepared well for the call. Call reluctance has been a problem when I started and even now.

I don't care to hear negatives. But I know when the prospect says no, he or she is saying, "tell me another reason why I should buy your product." I keep telling myself that I realize I haven't told the story enough times so that the prospect can understand it. To overcome call reluctance, be mentally alert, get enough sleep, be in physically good shape, and have knowledge of the product, tax laws, use of "vehicles" in order to advise the prospect how to benefit by their use.

Call reluctance diminishes as an agent gets more experience. I still feel it. It's there, but experience and knowledge are in your favor. The first call of the week, it's there. When an appointment is made, I feel more confident. The prospect is waiting for me. Call reluctance is tougher on cold calls, more so than on an appointment.

Building a Solid Relationship With the Client

When I make a sale, I generally suggest to my new client that we not lose track of each other. Part of my sale to him or her was based on the continuing service that I want to provide to each client. When I deliver the policy, I say that we will try to have a personal interview each year, even if for nothing more than a review and update of the coverages to see if the insurance plan is keeping up with inflation and *to see if it is still doing what it was meant to do at the time of sale.*

Read that last sentence again. Do you think you could work that philosophy into your delivery interview? Of course you could. It takes but a moment to express the thought, and it helps to build a more solid relationship with the client.

How many sales people do you know—of various services and products—who call you every year to see if what they sold you is still doing what you wanted it to do? As I review all the items I've bought in my lifetime, I have to admit no salesperson calls me on a regular basis to see if the product he or she has sold is still doing the job for me.

But you're an insurance agent, and the product you sell is designed for the approach of continuing service. A well-designed insurance plan can go out of date in a year's time, not through any fault of yours or of the client's. Things change. Inflation continues, and there may not be enough insurance dollars in the plan to do what the insured wants done. Beneficiaries and family situations change, and the settlement provisions may have to be changed. It's our job—our *opportunity*—to call again on our clients and offer to review the situation—to see that the plan is still doing what it was meant to do at the time of the sale.

These are the easy things in the insurance business, but yet the necessary things. It is these repeat sales that are easy because they come from the treasure chest of clients, and the field is always ripe and ready to harvest. That's why I have been such a firm believer in having a large base of policyowners that leaves me in the unique situation of never having to wonder where to go. As a result, 75 to 85 percent of my business each year comes from existing clients. These figures hold true even as I dictate these words: A large amount of the business that I wrote in the first part of this calendar year has again come from existing clients.

The Reapproach System

I think of calling on my clients as a "reapproach." I prefer not to drop in but to write a short note, followed up with a telephone call for the purpose of setting up an appointment. Again, my secretary is very valuable in setting up such appointments.

The ideas I use in this call are simple: a review of the estate plan, a review of business agreements, a review of the insurance in force—to see if these items have kept up with inflation, to see if they are still doing the job they were supposed to be doing a year ago.

I have never heard a client say to me, "I already bought life insurance from you," stating this as an objection. I have heard the objection, "I feel I have adequate insurance." And I think this is a legitimate objection. But when you analyze it, is it an objection or merely a statement, a statement made by a layperson who really doesn't know whether the insurance that he or she has is adequate or not? How seriously would a doctor take a patient's statement, "I don't think I have anything wrong," until the doctor has analyzed and diagnosed the situation? How seriously would a lawyer take a client's opinion, "I don't think this contravenes any laws or regulations," until he or she has thoroughly researched the situation?

Of course, there are times when a prospect knows that the insurance is not adequate, but has underlying reasons for not wanting to buy at this time. In these situations, the prospect may be reluctant to tell you the facts, the truth concerning why he or she doesn't want to buy at the present time. What client would want to tell you that a business is short of cash, or that he or she is having marital problems, or that some temporary business or personal stress is causing hypertension and the client, therefore, doesn't want to take an insurance medical examination?

Our skill as life insurance agents is to analyze what is happening when a prospect "objects." If I can find what the underlying cause of resistance is that causes the prospect to back up or to tell me that he or she has enough insurance, perhaps I can tell the prospect that I might be able to design a program with which he or she can obtain the amount of insurance really needed without a lot of additional dollar outlay. Or I may determine that the present moment is not the right time to attempt to sell new insurance and to withdraw gracefully until the time is more appropriate.

(I should note here that a good number of my clients will call me and say, "Don, we were thinking about . . ."—and it may be keyperson insurance, an estate plan, etc.—there are just so many things people think about, and if your name comes to their attention, they're going to give you a call. If you've done an honest job, if you've given good service, and if you're the kind of agent they would like to seek out, they'll call you.)

The Smorgasbord Approach

When I meet a prospect for the first time, I use the "smorgasbord" approach. That is, I like to go through several ideas rather than trying to zero in on one specific thought or need. By going through this approach, somewhere along the line of ideas my prospect will say, "Now that's something that I haven't given thought to" or "That's something I haven't heard of before." By doing this, the prospect tips his or her hand as I'm going through my assortment of ideas.

What are the ideas in my approach?

They're simply the ideas and general thoughts that most insurance agents would—and should—be discussing with a prospect. The ideas include the will of the prospect (and the spouse's will), taxes—and their effect on estate accumulation and conservation (during life and after death), his or her life insurance policies (how they are set up, whether they are designed to do the job that they are supposed to do), pensions for the business owner, deferred compensation, salary continuation, group insurance, the use of trusts, and so on. As I move through the line of ideas, something is sure to be of interest to my prospect, and then we have something tangible to talk about.

As someone who has sold life insurance, you know that we don't like to think that the prospect is going to resist the concept of life insurance or that he or she dislikes the people who sell life insurance. But we acknowledge that there are people with these thoughts.

So I like to convey to them that I have their best interests at heart—which I do. Their defense goes down, and their listening power comes up.

When we approach prospects about what they want for their families, we soon find that we are talking about the same thing. Not life insurance, but the *benefits* of life insurance. Since we're offering them something they already want, it shouldn't be hard to make them want it enough to put aside a little money each year to acquire it. On the initial contact, we are selling ourselves and our service—not life insurance as such. Prospects are people, and people can be funny. What makes sense to one doesn't necessarily make sense to another. Each has his or her own way of reasoning.

I have a sensitivity in the approach which lets me detect how the prospect is reacting to me. I can tell whether I am reaching them or whether they are leery of me. If I have the feeling that they are wary of me, I change my approach and may come right out and tell them that I have the feeling they are suspicious of life insurance and the people who sell it. I re-emphasize the fact that I am in their presence at the suggestion of one of their friends, that they needn't be afraid of what I am going to say, and that I am not going to sell them something they do not need or want to buy.

Probably one of our greatest weaknesses as agents is that we talk too much and listen too little. We seldom get the buyer into the act. That's why it's a good idea to have a series of questions ready on our initial call so that we can get a prospect to talk about himself or herself, and what he or she would like to accomplish.

It all boils down to communicating.

4.

INTERVIEW TECHNIQUES

Probably no component of the entire life insurance sales process is more important than the first interview. If the first visit doesn't work, there is no second interview. If what you accomplish during the first interview isn't good enough, your second interview will be ineffective. If you want to become a successful life insurance agent, pay special attention to what you do in that all-important first interview.

Five Objectives

Over the years, I have refined my first interview to the point where it accomplishes five objectives:

1. It establishes contact with the prospect. I will never sell life insurance to anyone until I have had the opportunity to sit down with him or her.
2. It lets the prospect see who—and what—Don Van Der Weide is. I am a soft-spoken, sincere, competent individual who wants to offer some help to the prospect and his or her family with estate planning matters.

3. It permits me to secure facts about the prospect and his or her financial and family situation to determine what need, if any, the prospect has for life insurance.
4. It sets the stage for the second interview and, when feasible, permits me to arrange a medical examination of the prospect.
5. It gives me the go-ahead to consult with the prospect's professional advisers and to get them into the act.

A Track To Run On

Remember when you first came into the life insurance business and your manager or general agent gave you a sales talk to learn. Some called it a "canned" sales talk, although management stressed that it was an organized presentation, a track to run on. Having nothing better, we took the sales talk, learned it, made some sales with it, and then gradually "outgrew" it.

Perhaps we became bored with the repetitiveness of giving the same talk. Perhaps we learned another talk from an agent in the office. Or perhaps we felt that as we became more experienced in the life insurance business, we could put aside the things we had learned in our early days and go on to something more in line with our new stature.

Most successful agents settle into an established procedure. Although they may not consciously think of it, the words they speak in a sales presentation fall into what we would call an organized presentation. They don't speak as if by rote, nor do the words sound parrot-like as they come out (and indeed they shouldn't), but the words do have an effect on the prospect and lead the interview in the direction in which the agent wishes it to go. These agents don't fly by the seat of their pants. If they did, they wouldn't be successful.

I have a track to run on, based on questions I ask the prospect. I am a great listener, and I ask questions which:

- show the prospect that I am there on serious business.
- indicate that this isn't a life insurance sales talk.
- give me the information I'll need to come up with a sound recommendation.
- permit me to "read" the prospect's attitude to me, and to life insurance.

The following is my track. I recommend it to you.

1. I thank the prospect for his or her time. Perhaps this is a type of small talk, but it expresses my attitude to the interview and to my relationship with clients. Although the interview will be of benefit to the prospect, it will ultimately benefit me, too, and for this I am grateful.

2. If the prospect has already indicated an awareness of an estate or business problem, I ask who alerted him or her to the problem. This brings out interesting information which will be valuable in your sale. The answer tells you something about the prospect, his or her thinking, the prospect's professional advisers, and relationship to them.

3. I tell the prospect that information is valuable to the solution of any problem. "If I'm going to do a lot of work for you, I've got to know the facts." If the prospect will not give me the information, I can be of no use to him or her. The answer I get reveals if I have control. If I can sense a rapport—that I have made a good impression, and our chemistries are in accord—I move ahead and start asking for the information I need to make proper recommendations. If the prospect balks, I have to ask myself if I really have control and if I have built

up sufficient prestige. If the prospect won't give me the information, there is something missing, something lacking, and I have to pack up and move on. I am not a mind reader or a magician. If the prospect won't give me information, he or she will never sign a life insurance application.

I want to convey a sense of excitement. I want to show the prospect that I have his or her best interests at heart. To do this, I have a positive mental attitude. I'm energetic and enthusiastic. If I'm tired, this lack of energy will soon show itself to the prospect and connote a lack of enthusiasm. I want to show that I'm sharp and alert. Then the prospect will sense the urgency of the situation, appreciate that he or she must do something about it, and want to do that something *now*.

4. What are the ages of the prospect and spouse? Appearances are deceptive, and a youthful looking prospect may be much older (or younger) than he or she appears. Also important is the difference in the ages of a married couple. How much longer might the wife live after the husband's death?

5. I ask about the children: names, ages, health. Most important is the situation of each child. Are they married? Are they happily married? Where do they live and what do they do for a living? Can they support their own families with their earnings, or are the parents "subsidizing" them? Are any of the children still being educated? How much longer will this go on? Do they own their own homes? What types of mortgages do they have? How about grandchildren: number, ages, situations?

At this point, you're really getting into a family tree of the prospect and spouse. Why does he or she build an estate and to whom does the prospect want it distributed? Aren't *your* children and grandchildren prominent in your estate planning?

6. Do the prospect and spouse each have wills? When were they drawn up? What are the details of the wills? How is property and income to be distributed? What do the wills say about trusts? Where are the wills located?

7. What business interests does the prospect own? How about the spouse? There is a tendency sometimes to think that the prospect has only one business interest and the spouse has none. The prospect who owns a hardware store in town may also own an interest in another business in town or outside of town. After the prospect has given me details about his or her business interest, I simply ask, "What other business interests do you own?" or "What other businesses do you have an interest in?" After I receive an answer, I record the information and ask again, "any other interests?"

When the prospect is the husband, I follow the same line of questioning about the wife's interests. The prospect may have several interests owned by his wife, and she may even be active in their management. Don't assume the wife is simply sitting at home doing housework. This is fallacious thinking and can turn off the wife who may be sitting in on the interview. Be sure your fact-finding is complete and balanced.

8. I follow up with detailed fact-finding about the businesses themselves:

a. What is the book value?
b. Where do they stand on retained earnings? Amount? Is there a problem here with excess retained earnings?

c. What type of life insurance coverage does the business have on key people?
d. What life insurance plans are in effect in the business? Does the prospect have a business continuation agreement? If so, how is it funded?
e. What are they doing about pensions? What types of plans? What type of benefits? Who's covered? Who's not?
f. What other assets does the business have? Cash? Stocks? Bonds? What else?

9. I ask about the prospect's personal asset picture. What personal life insurance does he or she have? What about group insurance? What about household goods? Securities? How many homes does the prospect own? Other real estate? Where are they located? Other assets?

10. I ask about a wife's assets. What does she own? Does she have any separate sources of income? How much life insurance does she have? What does *her* estate picture look like?

You'll understand that this fact-finding just isn't a question and answer session, with me posing questions and the prospect supplying the answers. It doesn't work that way. A lot of seemingly casual conversation enters into the process, and the prospect tells me a lot of things as he or she answers my questions. You learn which family members are in favor and which may be in disfavor. You learn how a prospect feels about business partners and a spouse. A lot of information comes out on the table as you talk.

It's important to know what the prospect and his or her spouse own. It's just as important to know how they want all this distributed after their deaths. So, during the question and answer process or after it, I get into other areas, things which are just as important.

"How do you want to care for your widow after your death?" The prospect may never have had such a question posed to him, and may have never thought about it.

"How long do you want to remain active in the business?" Another question which a prospect may never have pondered.

"Who will run your business after you retire or die? When do you think you'll retire? What if you can't?"

The wheels generally go around as you ask these questions. I ask the question and then keep quiet. My job is to stimulate thinking, not monopolize the conversation. As you do this, you feel somewhat like a psychiatrist who directs a patient's conversation, seeking clues to the solution of the problem. Or, more important, to get the individual to actually see the problem and to acknowledge that, yes, indeed, there is a problem.

I have a table showing the impact of federal taxes on an estate. I point to the amount of the tax that would be payable on an estate similar to the prospect's and merely note, "that's the part that isn't yours." Many people have a vague idea that there will be a tax payable when they die. Yet, few have any idea of the size of the tax, and few know the techniques that can be used to reduce the tax payable. This, basically, is our job in such interviews: to show the problems, to make them concrete, and to help the prospect to arrive at sensible solutions.

All through the interview, I've been looking for the prospect's "hot buttons." I look to see what interests and what dismays him or her. If the prospect's comments indicate that he or she wants a business interest to remain in the family, I know that a hot button is to show a way that this can be accomplished. If the prospect gets vehement about death taxes, I know that suggestions for reducing the taxes will be welcomed.

Other Interview Ideas

The interview can touch on other ideas.

For example, the prospect's estate may be very non-liquid. He or she may own the best property in the world, but the family may not keep it if it has to be sold to raise cash to pay death costs. Liquidity may be a very desirable goal for the prospect.

Has the prospect entered into a program of gift making? I explain the gift tax provisions of the law and mention that many estate owners make lifetime gifts. Such gifts can reduce the taxable estate and also provide the donors with the joy of seeing the recipients' gratitude.

An important part of my first interview with the prospect is getting the names of any professional advisers and asking the prospect to let them know that I will be contacting them in reference to matters we have discussed in the interview. I also tell the prospect that I have uncovered critical problems, time is running out, and that a specialist is needed. I have one in mind—an attorney who has been of great help to my other clients, and one in whom I have great confidence. Even though the prospect probably has his or her own attorney already, I stress that a specialist is needed and that the lawyer I recommend will work (for a fee) with the client's advisers.

This point is very important. The practice of law is so vast that specialists are needed for various problems. The situation is quite similar to medicine. We have general practitioners for "run of the mill" problems, but when a special problem appears, a specialist is called for and a general practitioner would be the first to admit it. In estate planning, with the drafting of instruments for businesses and personal problems, a specialist is needed. The legal fees involved are minimal compared to the benefits that can result.

I secure the prospect's agreement on this point. I get a commitment that the prospect will call and tell his or her accountant to cooperate with me when I discuss the case. And one final point: If I sense that the moment is right, I tell the prospect that, if insurance is recommended as part of the solution, it will be necessary for him or her to be examined by a company physician. I tell the prospect that my secretary will be calling soon to arrange a convenient time for this medical. If I have made a correct judgment of the situation, the prospect won't balk. If he or she does balk, I try to find out what the real objection is. If I'm moving a little too fast, I postpone the medical until another interview.

During the interview, I might drop in little "commercials" for life insurance. I might point out that insurance is excellent for providing liquidity at death and that estate assets can remain in the family's hands since life insurance dollars are paying death costs. I might touch on the discounting of future dollars via life insurance. If it appears that a business buy-out might take place, I talk about the virtues of life insurance in making dollars available for the buy-out. No hard sell—just a calm but enthusiastic discussion of the value of life insurance in business and estate planning.

As I'm leaving, I remind the prospect that my secretary will be in touch with him or her shortly and that I will be contacting the accountant. I promise that my secretary will type a list of the items we discussed today so that the prospect can talk with his or her spouse about them.

And then my secretary follows through with phone calls—to the doctor, attorney, and prospect. And I visit the accountant. At a point in time, when tentative solutions have been prepared, we will all meet at the attorney's office. I act as a catalyst. I bring people together. I get movement. I help solve their financial problems.

It's difficult to tell where a sale will go. It's difficult, too, to give a sample "second" interview. Some sales aren't closed on a second interview or on a third. One case took 16 interviews with the various parties. A lot of time, you say? Yes, it is, but this case produced $1,700,000 of life insurance, calling for $130,000 of annual premium—plus $200,000 of pension contributions. You get out of life insurance interviews what you put into them. Estate planning work calls for time, expertise, and experience. I can't think of a better way of selling life insurance.

My Way

My client wants it simple. My verbal telling is important. First, I gather all the facts, how properties are held, what the will says, trusts, personal and business assets—all this on a large yellow pad of paper. Then I want to hear the prospect's objectives or goals for the estate. At that point, I may suggest that after I review he permit me to try to put something together for him to help solve his problem. If I can obtain the instruments necessary (that is, life insurance), I'll get back to him. I return with the policy and review the problem so that he understands. Then he'll say, "I understand the problem, but what is the solution?" I present the answer. The client frequently says, "I presume you want a check for the plan you have put together." And I simply say yes.

5.

AN ACTUAL FIRST INTERVIEW WITH A PROSPECT

Perhaps nothing will make my initial interview clearer to you than a description of an actual first call on a prospect. Here's how such a call went recently.

Another agent, who lived several hundred miles away from my area but was visiting on vacation, asked me to visit a prospect of his, an old friend who lived in my community. The agent wanted assistance in trying to uncover possible insurance needs of his friend. The friend (we'll call him Jack) was a retailer of ready-to-wear goods.

Having an appointment (a definite must in this type of joint selling), we called on Jack at his store. He suggested that we have coffee in his office where we could talk undisturbed. As we settled down around a coffee table in his office, I made sure that the other agent sat next to Jack and that I sat across the table from them.

The first few minutes were devoted to casual conversation centering on Jack's family, how long he had been in business, and so forth. I then turned the conversation to the reason for our call.

"You know why we're here, Jack," I said. "I'd like to see if I can assist you with any estate planning or business planning matters. I know nothing about you. On the surface, you appear to be a very successful businessman, and no doubt you've done a good amount of business and estate planning already. Frankly, there may be nothing that I can assist you with.

"But I often find, in visits like this, that something is uncovered that may be of interest to you and to members of your family. What I find may be beneficial to you from a tax standpoint—either income tax or the federal estate tax.

"I have nothing prepared. I very seldom work with reams of illustrations, charts, papers, and the like. What I would like to do is to discuss your objectives. For example, what is it you want to achieve during your lifetime."

Jack was 39 years old. He told me that his goal was to retire at age 45. Since he knew I was coming, he had jotted down a list of the properties and businesses he owned or had an interest in. There were seven different business interests. Obviously, Jack was a bright, successful young businessman.

Planning for the Future

"Jack," I continued, "I'd like to talk to you about your objectives. For example, what are your desires concerning these business interests?"

Jack had seriously thought about his future and what he wanted to happen to his assets if he died while still a relatively young man. Regarding his ready-to-wear store, he said that he had considered selling a minority interest in it. As for the other business interests, some he wanted ownership to continue (with his wife), but if an interest was such that it should be disposed of, he'd like his wife to have cash paid to her for the interest.

We went down Jack's list, and I got more details concerning each one, including the dollar value of the interests. Jack then gave me a second list he had prepared. This one showed his wife's business interests and the percentage she owned in each one. Surprisingly, she had interests in five businesses on her own. Obviously, any planning would have to take into consideration her interests as well as his.

I asked Jack about their wills. He said that they were prepared about two years before, and that he would be happy to give me copies of the wills for my review.

I then asked about any and all business agreements he had with business partners, and he said that he would give me copies of these, too.

Professional Counsel

At this point, I got into the matter of legal and accounting assistance for Jack's situation. I told him that I would like to recommend a competent attorney to prepare any estate planning documents which might be necessary. I would also like to have his accountant present when the meeting with the attorney took place.

Jack asked me what I had in mind.

One thought I had, I said, could be an agreement exchanging stock he owned for cash payable to his estate.

Such an exchange might be able to be made on a favorable basis. Details, of course, would be left up to legal counsel.

I mentioned an irrevocable life insurance trust. A discussion of his life insurance policies had indicated that some insurance was owned by him, some by his wife, and some by his business. There was the danger that the life insurance could compound the estate tax liability problem at his or his wife's death. With proper planning, an irrevocable trust could substantially reduce the amount of tax payable at this death.

Jack thought for a few moments about the things I had discussed. Then he said, "Don, why don't you select the attorney? That sounds like a good idea. Then we'll get my accountant involved. Let's look into the irrevocable life insurance trust first."

That was the idea that appealed most to him, his hot button. With other prospects in similar situations, other ideas might prove appealing. The purpose of my mentioning several ideas in the interview was to see which way Jack wanted to go, what actions he wished to take, even if only on a tentative basis. Jack liked the idea of the trust, and this was the springboard to action and additional planning.

Jack commented that he had been called on by many life insurance agents, a natural occurrence since he was prominent, young, and successful—a natural prospect for life insurance sales people. These agents, however, had called on him armed with elaborate proposals designed in advance, although they knew nothing of his personal and business situation and could not know that any of their proposals would do what had to be done. Jack noted that if he took their proposals away from them, they would be completely off track. And they would be.

I find that my approach, asking questions and mentioning possible solutions, is readily accepted by businesspersons and other estate owners. It's low key, without pressure, and leads to an intelligent discussion of the problems facing the typical prospect I call on.

To finish the story of this first interview, I jotted down as a reminder the items I wanted:

Life insurance policies
Wills
Business agreements

Since Jack had asked me, I said that I would find a competent legal adviser to be of service to him in this situation. The interview was over. It had taken only 45 minutes.

During such an interview, I will frequently arrange for the prospect to take a medical examination to help determine if he or she can qualify for the insurance that may be recommended. In Jack's case, I felt that such a move would be premature and that it could be handled naturally on the second interview.

Some Power Phrases

As you can see, I'm not much for power phrases. My power comes in the approach, in the ideas presented, and in the solutions offered. However, let me pass along a few expressions accumulated over the years that I may use in an interview:

"Do you want the State and Federal Governments to dictate who is going to get what you have worked to accumulate over a lifetime? Why don't you put it all in writing and express your views and desires thoroughly? In that way, there will be no doubt what your intentions are. You can't put too much in writing while you're alive.

"You have silent partners. They'll all be there, with hands out when you die. There is a transfer tax waiting for you and me, a tax on the right to pass property to your beneficiaries. Before your beneficiary gets anything, Uncle Sam and the state in which you reside want a piece of action. I don't think you want these people to get any more than is necessary. Tax avoidance is perfectly legal—and proper. Would you be interested in a way to pass as much as possible at the lowest possible cost?

"There is a price tag on everything. There is the cost of doing something, and there is the cost of doing nothing. Take your choice. Either you do something about your situation or the government will do it for you. In many cases, the cost of doing something is far less than the cost of doing nothing.

"We can use your dollars to solve your problem, or we can use mine. Your dollars cost 100 cents each, and mine cost only pennies apiece. Whose dollars would you rather use—yours or mine?"

To recap what I did in my first interview with the prospect:

1. I made contact. By working with the other agent, I was able to gain entree to Jack.
2. I showed Jack that I was a competent individual who was sincerely interested in helping him solve some problems facing his estate.
3. I found out a number of facts about Jack and his situation, including securing copies of various documents relative to his current estate and business planning.
4. I set the stage for the next interview.

That's it. No miraculous feats, no spellbinding words. Just a simple track on which to run, with no solutions figured out in advance, backed up by cumbersome illustrations. It works well for me. It can work well for you.

6.

SOME ATTITUDES ABOUT LIFE INSURANCE SELLING

Let me start this chapter with a story. The story has a moral, and I think it will help you to better understand my approach to life insurance selling and service.

About 20 years ago, a lawyer in town did some work for me. As he concluded, he asked me to prepare an illustration for a $10,000 life insurance policy for him. I walked out of his office elated that a highly regarded attorney would ask a younger man for information about a life insurance policy. As I started to put something together for him, however, the thought crossed my mind that this really was not the right way to go about it.

Questions occurred to me like:

"Why just $10,000? Why not $5,000. . . or $50,000?"

"What does he have at present?"

"What does he need?"

I didn't want to go back to him without the figures, but I knew I had to.

I returned to his office and said, "If I requested you to draft a properly drawn will for me, could you do it without asking me some questions?"

His answer, of course, was no. "Well," I replied, "that's the situation I'm in right now. I can't make myself believe that you need a $10,000 policy—or one for $1,000 or $100,000—unless I have some questions answered."

Then I learned that he had already had proposals from other agents who said that they didn't need other information. I could tell that he was impressed with my approach, and he got the message. Several days later, I made a substantial life insurance sale. Little did I realize that this wasn't to be the whole sale but only the tip of the iceberg.

Several years later, this same attorney took in a partner and laid the groundwork for partnership and personal insurance on his new partner. In the years that followed, partnership insurance was added frequently on both men. Naturally, I pursued their personal programs and placed policies on members of their familes.

More years passed, and a third partner was added. Again, the same story. Two years after that, we put in a group insurance plan. A year later, they formed a professional corporation, and a pension plan was put into effect.

I think to myself from time to time: What if I hadn't taken the honest—and professional—approach and told my prospect that I couldn't make a sound recommendation for him if I didn't have more facts? During the years, I have heard these attorneys tell many clients, "We purchased our insurance from Don because he cared enough to determine what we needed and could afford."

Incidentally, this valued client refers me to 25% of my business year after year! Such is the value of the open and direct approach.

The Best Time To Sell Insurance

If I were to ask you to tell me some of the happiest moments in your life insurance career, I'm pretty sure that you'd relate a number of times when you had just closed a sale. The most vivid impression you would have, I know, would be when you had *just* closed a good-sized case. It might be the prospect who had held you off for a number of months or years and then finally signed the application. Or it might be your first big case.

These are happy moments, with you and the prospect sharing high emotion. You're elated that you've made the sale, and the prospect is happy that he or she has taken a big step toward solving a financial problem. You're both happy—and relaxed. What better time for you to start another life insurance sale.

Whenever I write an application, I like to plant some seeds with the applicant before I leave. I may have just written $50,000 of Whole Life on a farmer, with the insurance proceeds to provide estate liquidity. But he has many other needs which can be helped by life insurance, and I've made a careful study of these other needs in my fact-finding and sales process.

So I plant the seed of an idea with the client before I leave. It may be an idea on wife insurance. Sure, *he* has a pretty good life insurance program, but where does his wife stand? What would be the effect on his personal or business situation if his wife dies before he does? Of if his wife dies after him and after she's inherited a farm worth half-a-million dollars? How much life insurance does she have? How much does she need?

The idea might be insurance on the children. If a client believes in life insurance for himself or herself, the client should believe in insurance for the children. Life insurance for young people is a great deal: they're generally insurable, premiums are low, and guaranteed insurability options can be added to the coverage. Why not start their life insurance programs now?

The idea may be disability income or hospital expense and major medical coverages. As life insurance salespersons, we sometimes lose sight of our clients' needs for health coverages. What if the client doesn't die physically, but dies economically? What if he or she becomes disabled? What will happen to the beautiful estate plans that have been made? Where will income come from?

The Yellow Pad Technique

So here is what I do at the end of my sales interview, right after the prospect has signed the application. I carry a pad of yellow paper with me and use it during the interview to make points, do simple calculations, and so forth. Taking a fresh sheet of paper, I jot down on it one or two simple ideas. For example, if I'm thinking about insurance on the children, I'll write down two or three good reasons for its purchase. After writing down the points and briefly mentioning them, I hand the sheet of paper to the applicant, saying, "Fred, I want you to think about these things between now and the next time I see you, that is, when I deliver the policy to you. These are some very important things for you to consider.

Discuss them with your wife. I feel that if you give serious consideration to them and you're honest with yourself. You'll find that it will be of real benefit to you in the future."

When I deliver the policy, I bring up that particular idea or thought. Sure enough, Fred will often trot out that yellow sheet of paper and say, "Yes, we'd like to do it." The worst that he can say is, "No, we're not ready for it now."

If he says that, I ask, "When do you think you will be ready?"

Then I take out my appointment book and say, "Let me jot that down since my memory's shorter than a pencil. I'll be in touch with you then."

This technique of jotting down ideas on the yellow sheet has many advantages to you. There is no better time psychologically to bring up a new idea with the prospect than when he or she has just shown supreme confidence in you and your ideas by buying life insurance from you. And the prospect is relaxed since it's apparent that any selling on your part is now over.

As I've indicated, one of two things will happen: the prospect will say no to your ideas, or he or she will say yes. Even if the answer is no, he or she is not saying no forever. The client is simply saying no, not now. If you plant enough seeds, you'll find that some of them will grow, some will remain dormant for a while, but eventually most of them will sprout. The benefit of planting seeds is that *you develop a continuous ongoing procedure, and you will never have to start a repeat sale from scratch.* I truly wish that I had started planting seeds with people right from the start of my career in the life insurance business. If you're relatively new in selling, start this yellow pad technique today.

In order to be able to list the ideas on the yellow sheet, you've got to have a good knowledge of life insurance and needs for it, and you have to have done a thorough fact-finding job in your initial interviews. You've got to listen well during your interviews, not just to the prospect but to the spouse and any business partners. If the prospect indicates that he or she is unsure of his or her insurability status, that's a signal of a possible interest in guaranteed insurance purchases for the children. If the prospect wants to leave a business or farm intact to his or her heirs, that's a signal that life insurance for business and estate purposes is a good possibility. Listen for the signals that you are bound to get in any interview. Listen to the prospect talk. In many instances, it's more what the prospect says than what you say that will make the sale.

Rated Policies

I've received my share of rated policies during my twenty-plus years in the life insurance business. I'm sure you have, too. It's something one never quite gets accustomed to. Selling the prospect in the first place is generally difficult enough, but going back with a rated policy can frequently be a tough second sale. I do, however, have a philosophy which makes placing certain rated cases not that much of a problem. *The key is to make absolutely certain that your clients know and understand their needs for life insurance.*

Let me tell you about a recent case to illustrate what I mean.

I sold insurance to an individual who, as luck would have it, had high blood pressure, and this was picked up on the physical examination by the physician. In many life insurance situations, the agent is the one who tells the applicant of any physical problem and that the policy has been rated. *My procedure is different: I make sure I'm not the first person to tell the client about any physical problem.*

I've always asked the medical examiners in this area to do something when they check an applicant's blood pressure and find that the reading is above 140/90. When this happens, I ask them to indicate to the applicant that the blood pressure reading isn't "normal" in the eyes of my company and to point out that because it's not "normal," the policy may not be issued standard. It's as simple as that—and the information coming from the doctor has a lot more weight than coming from a life insurance agent.

If the policy that is issued subsequently is rated for blood pressure, I am in a different position when I deliver the policy. At that time, I ask "Did the medical examiner talk to you about your blood pressure?" The client admits that the doctor did bring the point up, and indicates that he or she understands that his or her blood pressure is not "normal" for life insurance.

I then tell the client that's so, that his or her health is not exactly perfect. But, I add, I'm pleased to say that the company did accept him or her as a life insurance risk and did issue a policy—*a standard policy in his or her health classification.* Isn't this great for the life insurance salesperson? You don't deliver the bad news that the applicant is not in good health (a physician has already indicated that the blood pressure situation is present). The applicant admits that he or she is not a super-risk, and then you say that you have a policy which is standard in his or her health classification.

I go on to explain what the policy means. Because of a blood pressure condition, his or her life expectancy—on the average—will not be as long as a person who has a normal blood pressure reading. Life expectancy might be, say, 20 years, as opposed to a person of the same age who has better blood pressure, who has an expectancy of 25 years. In this situation, wouldn't the client expect the premium rate to be different? Wouldn't he or she expect to pay somewhat more with a shorter life expectancy? Of course.

But his or her insurance needs, in spite of all this, are just as great, aren't they? In the case I mentioned concerning my client with high blood pressure, we were discussing a $50,000 sale of insurance in a partnership situation. I simply said, "We've discovered that your partnership needs $50,000 at your death, so your needs are the same. The only thing that has changed is that my company might have to pay this money out sooner than we had originally expected. Because of this, we'll have to put in a little bit more each year."

I tell my clients that I will work very closely with them. I request that they go to their personal physician. I tell them that if they follow their doctor's orders to the letter, it's possible that the insurance company will reconsider the rating in 12 months if their blood pressure is lower than it is now.

Before long, if the blood pressure is lowered and the rating is reduced (or removed), I have another sales opportunity. With their saved premium dollars, I can suggest that they buy additional coverage.

7.

HOW TO SELL PERSISTENT BUSINESS

Persistency is important to every life insurance agent. What's the sense of writing business if it won't stay on the books? Why go through all the effort we go through to find a prospect, to arrange an appointment, to make a presentation, and to close a case if the policy drops off the books in a month, six months, or a year? Our goal isn't to sell life insurance—it's to sell life insurance that will persist. If it doesn't, it's of no benefit to us, to our companies, and most of all—to the insured.

I can't give you a positive way to be sure that the business you sell will be quality business that doesn't lapse. But I've been in the business 22 years and my persistency rate ranges from 96 percent to 100 percent, and I can recommend a few things which may be of help to you.

Selecting Prospects

I believe the way you insure lasting business starts with the process of selecting a prospect. As you know by now, prospecting just isn't securing names of people. Prospecting is a selection process, a process of finding people not only whom you can approach and sell, but people whom you can live and grow with as clients. As I approach my prospect, the computers in my head are whirring as I weigh his or her potential as a member of the Don Van Der Weide clientele.

Who Can Afford It?

I want someone who can afford the life insurance I intend to sell. This is a very important characteristic not only in making the sale but in having the individual keep the insurance in force. This doesn't mean that the prospect has to be wealthy, since many of my cases are initially modest in size. I grow as my client grows. It does mean that the prospect has to have money to put into life insurance premiums—not just the first premium but all the premiums that will follow.

People today have money. Look at their homes, their cars, their lifestyles. The prospects I work with have money. My job is to convince them to "spend" some of that money on the life insurance I propose. The more effort you spend in finding people who can afford life insurance, the less effort you will have to spend later on in seeing that the insurance stays in force.

Who Needs It?

Another important consideration in qualifying the prospect is to find people who *need* insurance. Of course, everyone needs life insurance, but I'm more interested in specific needs for insurance that I can demonstrate. I have never tried to be a "policy peddler." I believe that it's my job as a life underwriter to uncover needs and then to demonstrate those needs to the prospect. Let's face it—most people are unaware of their complete needs for life insurance. Yes, they have a vague concept that life insurance is a necessary product and that everybody should own some. They know that life insurance can be used to provide cash at their death and to continue an individual's income to family members after death. But aside from these general thoughts about life insurance, most people are completely—and sometimes blissfully—unaware of their specific needs for life insurance. It's my job to uncover those needs and to point them out to the prospect. Why should the prospect buy anything he or she doesn't need?

In terms of persistency, it's important that the policyowner knows why he or she bought the insurance. If the policyowner thinks of the life insurance solely as a bill that pops up occasionally—and only in this regard—he or she will be more apt to drop the insurance whenever a premium payment is inconvenient or when some cash is needed. If, however, he or she knows that the insurance is the cornerstone of a family income program, an estate conservation plan, or a business continuation agreement, the policyowner will think twice and then again before entertaining a thought about lapsing the insurance. *This is a key point*: the prospect must know why he or she is buying the insurance (when buying it) and why he or she is maintaining it (as premium payments come due). It is the *need* for insurance that makes the program meaningful. People tend to hold on to what they need.

Overselling

Every sale we make is a fine balance between what the prospect needs and what the prospect can afford to pay. To do the best job for the prospect, we try to sell him or her as much insurance as is needed. The limiting factor is the amount of money the prospect can expend on premiums to continue the insurance. That is, all the life insurance he or she owns, not just the amount we have sold. Term insurance and permanent insurance each have their place in good insurance planning. If the right type of insurance is sold in the first place, the problem of overselling generally will not occur. If I've done my homework with the prospect and have had a personal visit concerning his or her needs, objectives, and desires, I can soon determine the type of insurance the prospect should have and can afford.

Another important point to keep in mind: If this is your first sale with the client, it probably will not be the last one if you do a good job of selling and after-sale service. You probably won't cover all of his or her needs on the first or second sale. A good client relationship will lead to more and more sales, and eventually you will sell all or most of the insurance the client needs. Don't try to sell everything the first time around; this is probably the greatest cause of overselling.

The Warning Signs

The warning signs of a lapse are found in the prospect before you even make the sale. I prefer not to spend time with people I know have trouble paying bills (this includes the unemployed and those who have trouble holding a job). If they can't pay the butcher or baker, why should I feel that they will pay their insurance premiums? I prefer not to spend time with people who aren't getting along with their business partners or with their spouses. Life insurance ownership involves continuing obligations and continuing responsibilities. If a business or marriage partnership isn't stable, chances are that the need for which the insurance is purchased will not be stable either.

These symptoms of future lapse can appear early in the prospecting and selling process. Listen to the prospect's comments, even those made jokingly, about bills, debt load, relationship with business associates, and feelings toward his or her spouse. These sentiments often come out in the form of objections to the interview, to life insurance in general, and to the specific plan you recommend. The insurance that is sold to such individuals is often lapse-prone.

Notice of Lapse

All right, let's say that you've done a good job of carefully screening your prospect and that you've demonstrated his or her needs in a competent and professional manner. The insurance is purchased and put in force, and you move on to selling other prospects. Then one day, an unwelcome piece of mail—a lapse notice—crosses your desk. Your policyowner has lapsed—or is about to lapse—the insurance you so carefully sold. What do you do?

What do *I* do? It's a simple procedure. First, my secretary gets on the telephone and calls the policyowner. In many cases, it's simply a matter of a mislaid premium notice or some confusion existing. My secretary's call uncovers what the problem is and usually gets the client to pay the premium. But what if it's something more important than the above reasons? This is where I get into the act.

I'll spend time with the client to see *why* the policy has lapsed. There are a number of reasons why I want to see the coverage reinstated, other than the loss of future commissions. I take great pride in the insurance programs I sell, and I want to see them carried out. I have great concern for the families and business associates of my insureds. A lapse signifies a breakdown in planning, and I want to get to the bottom of the situation.

When I contact the client, I ask if something has happened financially. If he or she is having temporary difficulty paying the premium, I usually can recommend a way out of the situation. Perhaps something has happened to the client's family situation, affecting the need for insurance. I find out what that change is and then analyze its effect on the program. Perhaps I oversold the client—not a pleasant thought to me or to any other agent. Perhaps we both were too optimistic at time of sale about his or her ability to continue the program. If so, what adjustments can be made now to save most of the program?

A Four-Step Plan To Reinstate

As you see, there are four simple steps to follow when you receive a lapse notice:

1. *Call the client immediately.* A lapse notice is an important communication and it should be followed up the same day you get it.

2. *Determine if the lapse occured and why.* Perhaps the client's check crossed in the mails and the lapse notice was simply a warning of sorts. But if the policy did lapse—or is about to lapse—determine the reason it lapsed.

3. *Help the client with a solution.* You know more about life insurance than your client does. You know the status of his or her dividend account, the amount of the cash and loan values, and the presence of the automatic loan provision in the policies. You know that annual premiums can be changed to semi-annual, or that semi-annual premiums can be changed to automatic monthly deductions from his or her checking account. You know that face amounts can be adjusted. Put your expert knowledge to use in saving the policy, using the same effort you used in selling the policy.

4. *Make a good effort.* A lapsed policy means less future income to you in terms of commissions from the policy. It may also mean that you will never sell the client again. Most important, it means no protection for the client. It means a family left unprotected or a business placed in a possibly hazardous financial condition when the client dies. This is the real loss involved in a lapse, and we as life insurance salespersons must do our best to reinstate lapsed policies.

As I noted at the start of this chapter, I have never had a lapse problem. Perhaps I'm one of the fortunate few, or perhaps it's due to the things I've mentioned in this chapter. I'll note one more thought that seems to have had an effect on the quality of the business I sell.

I've always tried to prospect vertically, that is, doing business with those more successful than I have been in life. The more successful I have become, the more successful the type of client I have sought out. Successful people have a way of getting things done. They seldom start something they don't finish. This is true of the life insurance they buy. My clients have made me successful by keeping the insurance I have sold to them.

Your clients can do the same for you.

My Way

One of the great paradoxes of our industry is that we can enrich ourselves by sharing. By sharing sales ideas and techniques with our colleagues, each of us becomes better at what we do and our whole profession benefits. And, more than that, we can share our dreams and motivations.

A special joy of my career has been sharing the insurance sales opportunity with others. I have introduced many agents to my company. As I helped others to succeed in the life insurance business, I found that I too enjoyed greater success. Helping others climb the mountain brought me closer to the top as well. I say it is a joy because when you bring sunshine to others, you can't keep it off yourself.

8.

WRITING FOUR TO EIGHT CASES A WEEK—EACH AND EVERY WEEK

There are a lot of ways to succeed in the life insurance business. Some people write lots of cases, some write large cases, and some write lots of large cases. I'm one of those who writes lots of cases, and every now and then I write some big ones. The combination has paid off well for me.

If I had to pick out a primary factor for my success through the years, I would have to choose Case Rate. There is no substitute for it, either for the new agent or for the established one. *The agent who writes several cases a week cannot fail in this business.*

There are four simple keys to building a large case rate:

1. *Prospecting.* You have to know how to secure the names of people who can buy life insurance from you.

2. *Client Service.* Once you sell a prospect, you have to keep in touch with him or her and render meaningful service.

3. *Time Control.* With the 101 things you must do daily, you have to control your time carefully to find, contact, and sell to people.

4. *A Specific Goal.* You must know how many cases a week you want to sell.

We've already discussed prospecting in Chapter 2, but let me add a few other points.

Don't Quit When You're Winning

Too often an agent is satisfied when he or she makes one or two sales a week. Too many agents let down too quickly when they make their quota of sales early in the week. It's a natural thing to do, especially in the life insurance business. It's a tough business, one that abounds in rejection. If we make one or two sales by Tuesday, why not relax and take it easy for a few days and then go to the wars again the following Monday? Although this line of reasoning sounds logical, it overlooks a fundamental point.

The more we sell, especially in a short period of time, the stronger we become. If we have our second sale by Tuesday, we're almost invincible for the rest of the week. Rejection means nothing—we've proved how good we are early in the week. Everything else that follows during the week is gravy. We become more relaxed, more confident and—most important—more aggressive. We dare to do better. . . We dare to tackle the tougher type of prospect. Our confidence becomes contagious. . . It's sensed by the prospect. . . And more sales follow.

If you want to write lots of cases, be sure you don't let up when the amount of sales you're satisfied with come early in the week. It's not wrong to repay yourself for excellent sales activity, but *don't do it at the wrong time*! Don't quit while you're winning! Make every hour, every day count when you're loose and relaxed.

Schedule the time off you wish to take. Schedule a week or two away with your spouse, and take that time when you've scheduled it. Let the time be your reward for what you've done in the past weeks or months. Just be careful when you choose to take the time.

You've heard the expression: The harder I work, the luckier I get. You've heard the term "momentum." When you work hard and build up momentum, you're setting up the machinery for accelerating your case rate. When you slack off and don't take advantage of the enthusiasm and momentum you've built up with a few good sales, you're impeding your case rate. If you want to have a high case rate, you've got to keep banging away when conditions are right for you.

Case rate becomes less of a chore once you've developed a clientele base. My clients are excellent prospects for me, especially those who already own substantial amounts of life insurance. They believe in life insurance, they have confidence in me, and I have no problem in getting to see them. What better type of prospect?

Some established agents eventually find themselves in the happy circumstances of securing 80% or more of their new business from their policyowners. I know I do. And that kind of selling is usually done in a relaxed, pleasant atmosphere. Compare the emotional environment you work in when you make your first call on a prospect. You're an unknown life insurance agent, there to sell the prospect something he or she doesn't want. The atmosphere is strained and tense. Compare this to a call on a client, especially one you've sold more than once.

You're greeted as a friend and trusted adviser. You're welcomed into the home or office and made to feel at ease. Gone is any suspicion of an unknown individual. They're dealing with a known and proven commodity. See how they introduce you to their children and business associates. There is respect, confidence, and friendship. All this comes from clientele building, and the basis of this building is case rate.

Client Service

Of course, all of this is predicated on the assumption that I've done a good job for my clients. Client service starts with selling the right plan and making sure that the plan continues to be the right one for the client. It means:

- Keeping in touch, taking care of beneficiary changes, following up any lapse notices which come along, and so on.
- Calling on the client from time to time and telling of changes that are taking place in the insurance market which might have some application to the client's situation.
- Calling on a rated policyowner to see if the rating can be removed or lessened.
- Sending birthday cards and age change notices, as well as the *Planned Financial Security* newsletter.
- Following up the guaranteed insurability options a client may have and making sure that he or she is aware of the great advantage such options offer.

- Doing all the things that another agent may not be willing to do or may not have the time or organization to do.

Client service, pure and simple, is hard work and it pays great rewards.

One reward is that you establish yourself as the client's life insurance agent. When life insurance is considered by the client or a member of the family, you're the one who gets called in. When a neighbor mentions life insurance, the client tells him or her about you and the type of work you do. The client is almost always available to see you when you call. Your ideas are listened to, your thoughts well-received.

My clients are believers in life insurance. They have bought good-sized amounts of life insurance from me, and they're well aware of the place of life insurance dollars in their estate plans and in their business situations. These people are well-to-do, and they expect their children to have similar estate and business needs for life insurance as they grow older. What better time to start their life insurance programs than now.

Fifteen percent of the insurance I sell is on young lives. The approach is a sound one and can be profitable to any life insurance agent. A million dollar policyowner buys $25,000 or $50,000 whole life policies on his or her children's lives and adds a guaranteed insurability feature. These policies extend the client base, adding young lives to help replace those lives which will not be buying insurance any more. One call on such a client may mean picking up three or four more policies, quite a boost to the case rate in one sitting.

You can increase your case rate by becoming more conscious of the insurance needs of the wives of your male clients. Forty percent of the insurance I sell is on these lives. Today's woman has substantial needs for insurance. If she is a wife and mother, insurance is needed to help replace the services she provides in the home. If she is a working mother, life insurance can help replace the income lost at her death. Insurance is needed on an estate owner's wife to protect the value of the marital deduction and to provide liquidity in her estate. By reviewing your client files right now, I'm sure you'll find quite a few policies you can write this year on clients' wives and children.

And don't overlook such products as health insurance policies, plans which will pay the insured an income when disabled or provide dollars for medical expenses. We sometimes lose sight of the need for health insurance by concentrating too much on life insurance. Complete financial protection involves providing for the risk of disability.

Selling life insurance to business owners leads automatically to selling insurance on employee lives with such protection paid for by either the employer or employee. When I make a sale to the owner of a business, I have a natural entree to his or her place of business. I can propose insurance on the lives of key people. I can recommend a payroll deduction plan for helping employees to round out their personal insurance programs. I can generally get to see employees during office hours to discuss their financial needs. All this is possible when the client has confidence in you.

One last thought about clients. They are excellent centers of influence for you. When the subject of life insurance comes up, I like to know that my clients will mention me as their insurance agent. Even if they only recommend me for sales to their spouses and children, that's fine. But when you've done a good job for them, you find that they will recommend you to many other people. And thus your circle of clients expands and expands.

Time Control

The next point to consider is how do you find time to sell so many people? One answer might be *you have time for anything, if not for everything.* Think about that for a minute. Every day we make choices by the minute and by the hour. We all have the same amount of time—24 hours a day. Some of this time must be allotted to sleeping and eating. Some is devoted to leisure and relaxation, and the rest is used in working. The difference in the success achieved by agents is generally found in how they spend their working hours. If you want to write a lot of cases a week, you must consciously choose to spend as much of your working time as possible in front of people who can buy life insurance from you. It's as simple as that.

I find that two keys to high case rate are *organization* and *simplicity.*

In my chapter on secretaries, I make the point that I never do what someone else can do for me. I have this perfected to a science. I do only what I alone can—and should—be doing. This point is difficult for some salespeople to accept.

We go back to basics. Why do you get paid? You get paid for selling life insurance. You do not get paid for answering phones, for checking your ledger, for checking your office's files on a client, or for writing business checks. You get paid for writing an application which the prospect will sign and for putting into force insurance on his or her life. Your efforts, therefore, must be devoted primarily to getting in front of people who will buy more insurance. No agent will ever get to the point where he or she spends 100 percent of available time in front of prospects, but you must get as close to 100 percent as your organizational ability and talent will permit you.

Simplicity refers to the type of presentations I make. I have never been one for long, fancy, exhaustive proposals. Yes, I know agents who are very successful who call on a prospect with proposals ranging up to 100 pages in length. These are beautifully typed and well-documented, and they take days or weeks to prepare. They call for much of the agent's time to devise and check, even when he or she has a staff assisting in such preparation. I'm not being critical of such presentations. They just don't work for me. I prefer plain, down-to-earth language and straight eye-to-eye presentations.

Perhaps it's the market in which I work. Perhaps it's just me. I like things to be simple. I like presentations that are easy to understand. The easier they are to understand, the more apt the prospect is to buy them. Although I'm a CLU, I don't want to present an idea to a prospect in such a way that only another CLU could understand it.

Perhaps it's the age of computers in which we live. Before computers came along, it was quite a chore for an agent to prepare a lot of figures for a prospect, and so the agent prepared only a few and centered on those few in the presentation. With computers, we now have hundreds of individual figures to show the prospect and thus we may be tempted to overwhelm the prospect with statistics. If we do this, he or she becomes confused. A confused prospect is not an about-to-buy prospect. He or she wants time to think it over, time to run the 101 figures past an accountant (who may be overwhelmed, too).

If you don't spend time on preparing exhaustive proposals, you have time to call on more prospects. If you can give a sales presentation in 10 minutes instead of two hours, you have more time to call on other prospects. If the prospect can understand your presentation and doesn't have to "think it over," you'll have fewer call-backs. With fewer call-backs, you'll have more time to call on other prospects. Have I made my point? By accenting simplicity, you can have a higher case rate.

Make It a Goal

This leads me to my fourth point: If you want a high case rate, you have to make it a goal for yourself. You can achieve just about anything you want to, but you have to know what you want to achieve. Years ago, I set out with a high case rate as a goal. And it has done wonders for me.

To improve your case rate, first determine what your case rate now is. How many policies did you sell last year? The year before? How many cases have you sold to date this year, and what does your projected annual rate look like? While you're calculating this, let me throw in some food for thought.

My company's statistics indicate that the more successful an agent is, the more cases he or she writes. By surveying the various "clubs" an agent can qualify for, it was shown that case rate increased dramatically with the club. Successful agents have high case rates.

Back to *your* case rate. What do you want it to be? Let's say you want at least 100 cases a year. That's just two cases a week—so your goal is a simple one. In addition to the other goals you have in life, you are now aiming for at least two cases a week. You won't stop working until you have those two cases. I wish I could give you some inspired thoughts or magical directions, but it doesn't work that way. If you want a higher case rate, just pick the case rate you want and set out to achieve it on a weekly basis, each and every week.

Goals are a good way to motivate yourself, and I can't think of a better goal than a specific case rate.

A high case rate means you're serving your community well. Once the life sustaining necessities have been met and some reasonable savings set aside, almost everybody has some insurance needs. That goes for the farm hand or factory worker who's making $8,000 or $10,000 a year as well as for the doctor or lawyer who's making 10 times as much. If we don't cover the insurance needs of those with modest incomes, who will?

I sell a few big cases a year, as well as a whole lot of little ones. I'm just as glad for the opportunity to help a family with a modest income as one with a large one. The numbers may be smaller, but the need is every bit as great. An otherwise penniless widow needs the insurance proceeds at least as much as a wealthy one. By reaching these prospects and selling them the same high quality products, and furnishing the same top-flight service, we're doing ourselves, our company, and our industry proud.

My Way

A growth process is constantly going on. You can't see a plant grow, but you know that a change is occurring. The process is slow, but the important thing is that it is always taking place. It is the same way with growth in the life insurance business. Everything doesn't happen overnight.

9.

AVOIDING OR OVERCOMING SLUMPS

Breathes there an agent with soul so dead who hasn't said: "I'm in a slump—how do I get out of it?"

Slumps seem to hit everyone who has to perform every day. We have good days and we have bad days. When the bad days appear to line up in a row, we're apt to say that we're in a slump. Slumps sometimes are easy to get into and hard to get out of. If it's any consolation, just about everyone gets into a slump—and slumps are relative. If some agents don't write an app in two days, they're in a slump. With others, it's two weeks. There are many reasons for slumps and thus many cures. The purpose of this chapter, therefore, is to examine the logic—or illogic—of slumps and to see what we can do to avoid them or to overcome them.

Boredom

Part of the slump syndrome is boredom. Once you get past the growing pains of life insurance selling, you realize that you've mastered the procedures necessary for getting prospects, interviews, and applications. You find that you no longer have a problem selling insurance—and a certain boredom sets in.

Think back to your earlier days of life insurance selling. Remember the kick you used to get each time you wrote an app? Remember the high you'd feel when you met a goal of, say, 10 apps a month? Remember the thrill of a larger than normal commission check when you made a "big" sale? As the months and years went by, the excitement died down, and the "thrills" seemed to come fewer and farther between.

When an agent is bored by a seeming lack of accomplishment, he or she starts looking elsewhere for *fulfillment*. That fulfillment may come in a number of ways. It may come through extra hours spent at a hobby, doing something one is good at, something which is pleasurable. It may come from civic work, chairing a committee involved in an important project. It may be found in whacking a golf ball around a course and breaking 80. The important thing to realize is that the fulfillment is being found *away* from the normal workday, with hours spent on areas other than business. Suddenly the agent finds himself or herself in a slump and wonders what happened.

Fulfillment is a necessary thing with humans, and we shouldn't disregard it. But we should seek to find fulfillment primarily in our profession. We can find it by stretching and by challenging ourselves. If an agent gives the same type of sales presentation day after day, he or she is bound to be bored. If an agent is still working exclusively in the same market in which he or she started, of course the agent will be bored. If an agent is selling the same type of policy with which he or she started, touching on the same basic needs, it's only natural that this agent won't find fulfillment. Growth is vital to prevent boredom.

Growth is found by increasing the knowledge necessary to work effectively in many markets. Enrolling in CLU studies is one way to achieve such growth. The study involved can provide freedom from boredom as well as an avenue to more complex, more interesting markets. Fulfillment comes more often by mastering the material found in the assignments, as well as from passing the examinations. The important point is that the agent must grow, must reach out, must become more capable of handling the financial needs of an increasingly sophisticated clientele.

Too Much Detail Work

Another reason for a slump is that the agent does more and more things he or she shouldn't be doing at all. The point is stressed several times in this book that all you get paid for is selling. When an agent brings in the mail from the outside office, opens it and goes through it, he or she is wasting valuable time. When an agent checks a file for a piece of information or makes a phone call to a company service office personally, the agent is doing things he or she is too highly paid to do. In some cases, it's hard to tell which came first: Is the agent in a slump because he or she is doing the wrong things, or is the agent doing the wrong things because he or she is in a slump?

Activity—doing something—is important to our peace of mind. When we're selling, we have peace of mind because we have tangible proof that we're doing something, something important, something which will give us an income, something which will reassure us. When we're *not* selling, it's important that we do something to give us a sense of activity. Thus, we may "go through the files" or "check the mail," anything to keep us busy and keep our minds off the fact that we're not bringing in applications. The trouble is that we're doing the wrong things. We should leave the paperwork to others and get out in front of prospects and ask them to buy. This is how slumps are broken—or eliminated entirely.

But, you say, I have a lot of clients, including businesses and pension plans. These people need service. There's a lot of paperwork involved. And to this I say fine, give your people the service they need. But do it through a secretary or administrative assistant. You'll be paying their salaries by the sales you're making while they're processing your paper.

Getting Stale

Slumps take place when an agent gets stale, and this staleness can be caused by a number of factors:

1. The agent is physically rundown. Perhaps he or she is overweight, smokes too much, or isn't getting enough exercise.

2. The agent doesn't enjoy what he or she is doing. It may be the market or it may be the limited type of sales presentation made to most prospects.

3. The agent is bogged down. Perhaps he or she spends too much time at the business of life insurance, and not enough on hobbies or recreation. One day fades into the next, and life isn't much fun.

The cures for staleness are obvious.

Being in good physical shape is a mental turn on for yourself and for your clients. You glow with good health, you're enthusiastic and confident. You just feel good all over. You've got plenty of pep in the morning and enough strength to carry you through late evening appointments.

You've got to enjoy what you're doing or you won't do it well. You've got to enjoy the challenge of selling, and you have to be able to put rejection in the proper perspective. You've got to like people—calling on them, talking with them, discussing their situations, and recommending solutions to financial problems. If you're not comfortable with these facets of life insurance selling, the chances are you don't enjoy what you do. If this is the case, you had better analyze why you don't.

In the pursuit of success, we sometimes spend too many hours a day working, eventually blunting the sharp edge we should bring into selling. Every now and then, we have to back away from our business and do something else, something different. No one can work continuously. A change of pace has to enter our workday or workweek.

Other Businesses

A slump can also occur when the agent gets too involved in other businesses. He or she makes money by selling life insurance and then turns to ways to invest that money. Investments may take the form of buying and selling securities or dealing in real estate. Instead of starting the day reviewing which prospects to call on and what ideas to present, the agent finds himself or herself reading the *Wall Street Journal*, plotting the buying and selling for the day. Instead of calling prospects, the agent is on the phone with his or her broker.

You tell yourself that you're becoming more of a businessperson, that you're growing financially and extending your sphere of influence. Sure it's fun to try your hand at making more money, but when you forget your major business—and the income *it* produces, you may find yourself in a slump. The problem is that you have moved away from your primary livelihood, the source of most of your income, and this neglect shows up in the form of a slump. When you neglect the business of finding prospects, making appointments, and making sales presentations, it's only natural that your production will suffer. We call it a slump and wonder why it happened.

Another reason for a slump is that you may have moved too far away from basics. Remember when you first came into the life insurance business and learned the basic needs people have for life insurance. You called on people with almost apostolic zeal and made sales. You were enthusiastic about life insurance, what it is, and what it can do. As time went by, your enthusiasm lessened and you became more "sophisticated." You drifted away from the basic needs and perhaps got involved with one or two "sophisticated" types of plans which intrigued you. Your fascination carried over to your presentation and you were able to enthusiastically recommend these new plans to prospects. But at some point in time, you may have to review what you're selling, what you're recommending to prospects and see if it is still sound basic life insurance. If not, you may be on your way into a slump.

Complacency

Still another reason for slumps is complacency, possibly demonstrating itself as an "I'm doing all right" attitude. An agent sets goals early in his or her career and accomplishes these. The goal may be 10 applications a month or $5,000 in annualized premium a month. It may be membership in the MDRT. When the goal is reached and new and higher goals aren't set, complacency can set in. The agent continues to attempt to write the number of apps he or she was originally challenged by. Or the original premium amount. Or MDRT membership. Or whatever the goal was.

But the goal is no longer enough, even when the agent continues to achieve it. Satisfied with the goal, the agent begins to slip back. Prospecting is no great chore. Calling prospects is not difficult. Asking people to buy is no staggering task. What isn't done today can be done tomorrow. Or next week. Life is good—and easy. So why aren't the apps coming in?

In our business, we have to run a little scared. We have to be eager for the next case, eager to replace a prospect who says "no" or even says "yes." We can't stand still, especially as inflation erodes our true income and as we desire a better standard of living for ourselves and our families. We can't afford complacency, nor can we afford settling for last year's standards.

Slumps can also be caused by personal pressure. It's difficult to be a sensitive, creative person in the type of work we do and then turn off that sensitivity when it comes to personal relationships. If a spouse is sick or a child is in trouble, it's difficult to wipe these things out of our minds and to concentrate 100 percent on the business of selling life insurance. Perhaps the best approach is to try to separate your business and personal lives—to concentrate strictly on business during working hours and, in turn, to concentrate on your personal and family relationships when you are not working.

You can't sell a cent of life insurance when you're sitting in your den watching television with your loved ones. You can't impress a client when you're playing catch with a son or golf with a neighbor. In the same vein, you can't help your child with his or her school grades while getting ready to call on a prospect. You can't call back an unkind word to a spouse as you work on the figures of an estate planning proposal. The key is to separate these two sides of your life. Following the good advice of "rendering to Caesar," we should give to our business 100 percent while involved with it and give 100 percent to ourselves and family and friends while with them.

Trying Too Hard

Strangely enough, another cause of a slump is "trying too hard." Sound strange—"trying too hard"? In sports, this may be called "pressing." The ballplayer who hasn't had a hit in a while starts to press. The hockey player who hasn't had a goal does the same. The muscles tighten up, and the athlete pays too much attention to the mechanics of the situation. Result: no hits, no goals. The same thing can be true of the life insurance agent.

A sale hasn't come along in a few days—or in a few weeks. It's natural to tighten up a bit when making a telephone call to a prospect. It's natural to press a bit when asking a prospect to buy. It's natural to try a bit too hard in getting a sale when one hasn't come along in a while. The agent becomes a little less objective and a little more subjective. That's the price you pay when you try too hard. You tend to think more of yourself and your objectives than you do of the prospect and his or her needs.

If you had been picking up sales at the accustomed pace, you wouldn't be trying too hard. "Failure" would be a lot easier to take. The cure for trying too hard seems to be contradictory: Sell more cases so you won't press so hard when you're not selling. Such is the logic of slumps.

To keep out of slumps, set an *exciting* goal. Make it something worthwhile, noteworthy, something you really have to stretch for. For example, plan on selling one million dollars of insurance in a month. For one month, aim to work like an individual who sells $12,000,000 of insurance in a year.

Following Ben Feldman's tip, break your goal down into workable pieces. On a weekly basis, you have to sell $250,000—a little more than $30,000 in a day. Before you start your month, plan your prospecting. Whom can you call on to sell a total of one million in a month? What prospecting and organizational activity will be needed before the month? What idea—or ideas—can you present to make the necessary sales? Will you use direct mail? Do you have a lot of term insurance on clients which can be converted? What will be your plan of attack?

Make up your mind that for one month you're going to run at top speed and plan your time schedules accordingly. Let certain people know about your goal—such as your spouse, your manager, your secretary. They'll become a cheering section for you and will spur you on in a number of ways.

Turning Inward

To overcome a slump, you have to identify the cause of the problem. What takes place frequently is that a person's thoughts turn inward. You spend so much time thinking about yourself and your own problems that you fail to think about others—especially prospects and clients—and their problems. You begin to feel sorry for yourself and your mind starts to send signals to your body. You don't feel very well. Perhaps you shouldn't try so hard. Perhaps you should take a few days off. Perhaps you should even try a different line of work.

You are "out of rhythm." You fret and stew. You look for someone or something to criticize. You criticize the company and its products. You criticize the manager and the office staff. You even get down on the economy, the government, or inflation. Or you get down on the whole business—people don't really want life insurance so why are we trying to sell it to them?

What can you do?

First, analyze the situation. What is the cause of this negative thinking and this lack of accomplishment? What are you really thinking about and what are you doing to yourself?

Next, get rid of the negative thinking that's clouding your mind and forget about yourself.

Positive thinking is better than medication. Start to think happy thoughts. Go over the good things in life that have happened to you and are still happening to you. In short, count your blessings. Get your mind full of healthy thoughts, let them sink in, and then see the effect these thoughts can have on others. When you're thinking happy thoughts, you'll be amazed at how you influence others. If you think right, you'll live longer and you'll be happier and healthier.

Get rid of the idea that selling life insurance helps you in terms of commissions. Start each day with the idea of helping others. What you do, what you say will be of great help to every person you call on during the day. When you start thinking more about others, you'll be amazed at how this attitude will help you. You begin to look happy. You *are* happy. Now you're living. You've allowed peace to come into your life.

I've found that my personal goals include:

1. Being loving toward everyone.

2. Being in tune with the created order around me.

3. Assuming high-level goals in terms of production.

4. Increasing my expertise—knowing what to do and when to do it.

5. Moving others—prospects, clients, associates—to higher goals.

6. Being a strong, ethical, healthy, wise, free person.

Perhaps the best solution for slumps is being willing to pay the price. That's what this whole book is about. When you do the things you have to do in this profession, you pay the price. Paying the price is the best way to avoid a slump.

My Way

One of the delights in selling insurance is that you develop your own work schedule. It has been said that organizing one's time is the key to success. In setting up a schedule, adequate time must be allowed for study, prospecting, and interviewing. By developing a habit of coming to the office at a certain time each day and by going through a planned routine of work, you find that time is of the essence and that you will accomplish more than you would otherwise. Also, by allocating a specific time each week for recreation, you will find that you will enjoy that period more. It becomes a reward for working instead of an excuse for not working.

10.

GUIDELINES FOR A NEW AGENT

From time to time, I'm asked by new agents for advice. The matter is generally posed to me in this fashion: I'm starting out in the life insurance business. Don, you've obviously been successful in this business, so you must know what you're doing. What can you say to help me achieve a measure of the success you've had?

It's always flattering to be asked for advice. No matter how experienced you are, it's rewarding to have someone ask you for guidance. With the outstanding men and women coming into the life insurance field today, it's a privilege to play some small part in their future accomplishments.

Whether talking to these individuals separately or as a group, I find that my remarks center on seven areas. Here they are.

Work Hard

Work hard. No one will ever succeed in the life insurance business without working hard. This guideline frequently sounds too pat, too glib. *Work hard.* Doesn't everyone work hard? My 23 years of experience have indicated that there is a difference between "working hard" and "working hard." Confused? Let me explain.

Joe gets to company's office at 9 A.M. His first order of business is to open the coffee container he's brought in and to pour in an appropriate amount of sugar. This is a welcome ritual for Joe, and he enjoys it. As he slowly drinks his coffee, his mind runs over a blur of details, of things done yesterday and things to be done today. He's getting organized. By 9:20, he's finished his coffee and goes to the washroom to freshen up. Finishing that chore, he goes to the front desk of the office to pick up his mail. He runs into Sam and Charlie, two fellow agents, and they discuss the basketball game that was on TV the night before. It's good-natured banter, and this fellowship is one of the main reasons Joe stops at the office each morning.

He returns to his office with his mail and goes through it. There's a policy that has just been issued standard (good news), a lapse notice (no way to start the day), two bulletins from the home office, the company magazine for agents, two bills for direct mail he sent out last week, and an advertising flyer. He returns to his office and drops the mail on his desk. He makes a mental note to call the new insured to arrange a delivery interview, as well as calling the lapsed policyowner in an attempt to reinstate the policy.

His eyes fall on the cover of the magazine, and he notes that this issue contains pictures of the company convention he attended a few months ago. He turns to the appropriate page and looks over the pictures, finding himself in a group photograph. There's a story accompanying the pictures, and he reads this, enjoying the memories that float back. It was a good meeting. Good times, good friends.

Finishing the magazine, he picks up the two direct mail bills and reviews the figures. Did he really send out that many letters? Did he specify first class postage? He could swear he had asked for third class. He'll have to check this.

By now, it's 11:40 and his mind turns to lunch. He wonders if Sam and Charlie are still in the office. He'd like to go over to the new restaurant on Main Street and see what the food is like. He leaves his desk and heads to the offices of the two other agents, thinking that after lunch he'll have to get on the phone and start rounding up some business.

We'll leave Joe at this point. Joe feels that he's worked all morning, and in a way he has. But let's compare Joe's morning to that of Chuck, another agent in the office who believes in working hard.

Chuck has a breakfast appointment with a possible new client at 8:30 A.M. The appointment runs about 45 minutes. Although he makes no sale, the client looks promising and may buy in a few months. Because of Chuck's presentation, he secures four referred leads.

As he leaves the prospect, he calls the office and speaks to Anne, his secretary. Anne has picked up the morning mail and has determined which matters require Chuck's personal attention. Coincidentally, Chuck's morning mail is the same as Joe's. Let's see how Chuck and Anne handle such matters.

"The policy on Jack Smith came in," Anne advises Chuck. "I'm calling his office a little later to arrange a delivery interview." Anne maintains Chuck's appointment schedule and knows where he'll be at all times.

"There was a lapse notice on Frank Hanley," she continues. "I called him and there seems to be a mixup in the company billing this month. Mr. Hanley sent the check in about two weeks ago, so I'm going to check with the Payment Office and get it straightened out. I told him I'd confirm his payment later."

"Good. Anything else?" Chuck asks.

"Not really. Some bills I'm going to check out, two bulletins from the home office, and something that looks like junk mail." Anne has already placed the last three items in Chuck's take-home file, and he'll go through them while watching television that evening.

"Okay, Anne. Since I don't have to be at the Johnson interview until 10 A.M., I'm going to stop in at Sue Miller's office and pick up the policies I told her we'd review. You can call me there if you need me. After Johnson, I'm going over to Hill City for that lunch date. I have a reservation at the Silver Cafe, don't I?" Anne confirms this, and Chuck goes off to see Sue Miller.

As you can see, Chuck has had a busy morning. By the end of lunch, he will have had three selling interviews in addition to a service interview. If Anne needs to get in touch with him in a hurry, she knows where to call. She also knows that he'll check in throughout the day. And notice how involved Chuck *didn't* get with the routine work that didn't call for his personal attention.

I won't belabor the point. I won't ask you which agent "worked hard" that morning. What type of hard work do you want to do? Joe's or Chuck's? Which will pay off for you and your family, as well as for your clients and your company?

Since many agents are satisfied with a lower standard of living than other agents, their hard work doesn't have to be as hard as that of other agents. How much do you want to succeed? That's how hard you have to work.

CLU Study

Become a CLU. After you've completed your company's training courses, go on to CLU study. There is no substitute for it.

Why study CLU?

The life insurance business is so complex today that knowledge is the key to bigger sales and better service to your clients. Yes, you still have to be able to sell, but you must have the goods to sell. *Ideas* sell life insurance; the better your warehouse of ideas, the better you'll be able to sell.

CLU offers an organized, paced study program. It should be approached as a way of becoming a more capable life underwriter, and the appropriate time should be put into it. Although there may be some CLUs around who did it by last minute cramming, the only worthwhile way to become a CLU is through constant (almost daily) study. Enroll in an organized class, if possible. If not, see if you can do it via correspondence courses. Buy the books and follow the study format provided in the CLU study guides. Do some studying every day.

You may find, as I did, that the CLU designation is just the start of a life long pursuit of knowledge in the life insurance business. CLU prepares you for this pursuit and provides a foundation for future continuing education. Without CLU studies, attainment of higher, specialized knowledge is almost impossible.

CLU makes you more confident. Some agents fear calling on prospects with higher incomes or specialized needs for insurance. Why? Because they feel that they will appear ignorant and incompetent—and possibly they will. When you're armed with the knowledge supplied by CLU, it is a rare prospect who can present a situation that you cannot discuss intelligently and suggest solutions.

CLU provides you with credentials in the business and professional communities. CLU marks you as an individual who has paid his or her dues and who is serious in a commitment to serve. It shows that you are a career life underwriter, capable of providing professional service to all. It is an entree to the solid, profitable markets in which you must work to achieve true success.

CLU makes your life more interesting. Let's say you decide to forgo CLU studies and to continue selling life insurance pretty much in the same way you've been doing since you entered the business. A human being needs a challenge in order to grow. When you do the same thing day after day, you become stagnant and bored. Life is dull, uninteresting. One of the joys of this business is the mental stimulation it can give: working with all types of people, all types of problems. Each situation is different, each solution is different. CLU lets you become more capable of working with many types of prospects and their professional advisors. It lets you keep up-to-date with the almost daily changes that are taking place in our world.

Night Work

Don't shirk night work. I don't recommend night work as a steady diet, but it may become necessary, especially in your early years. There may be some clients you can't see during the daytime and who must be seen at night. Life insurance selling isn't a 40-hour a week job. What successful person do you know who works only a limited number of hours a week?

Life insurance offers you the freedom of choosing your own hours. You don't have to work every night in the week, and you don't have to stay out all night working. When you do work an evening, you can arrange your schedule so that your first appointment the following morning is at a later time. If you're married, you have to consider your spouse. Perhaps you can set aside at least one evening a week to go out with your spouse while limiting your evening calls to a specific number of nights each week. In this way, your spouse will be able to adjust to your absence from home some evenings.

Even now, I do a limited amount of night work. Not often, I admit, after all these years, but such appointments have led to some interesting cases.

Hire a Secretary

Hire a secretary. You're a *salesperson.* You get paid only when you sell. Your company doesn't pay you to make telephone calls, to send out direct mail, to check records, and the myriad of things a secretary can—and will—do for you. Again: you're paid only to sell. Your commissions are based on sales you make. Everything else is secondary.

Remember Chuck and his secretary, Anne, in the above example. Let's return for a moment to that case so I can make a point or two:

1. Chuck spent his whole morning with prospects and clients. He had no reason for coming to the office.

2. Anne gave Chuck all the information (and *only* the information) he needed.

3. Anne did valuable service work for Chuck. She called clients to arrange delivery interviews and to check into lapsed policies. She took care of his paperwork and business expenses. She separated the wheat from the chaff. She gave Chuck valuable time. With this time, Chuck was a better salesman. He could make more sales presentations to more people. His mind wasn't cluttered with details that didn't call for his talents.

4. She relieved Chuck of all things which an agent can use as an excuse for not selling. We sometimes see agents who confuse activity with work. If they spend a morning in the office shuffling papers, they feel that they have worked a morning. Not so.

The Annes of this world are tremendous assets to those of us who sell life insurance. You can't really succeed without a secretary. Without one, you'll never reach a professional level. What doctor or lawyer do you know who handles his or her business records, types letters, and so forth? Enough said. You need a secretary. The freedom a secretary will give you will more than repay the money paid in salary.

Set Goals

Set goals. Don't float through life, hoping that your ship will reach success. If you want to get someplace, you have to know where you want to go in order to get there. Set goals: short-term, intermediate, and long-term. And set them high. Be sure you have to stretch for the goals. Even if you fall short of your high goal, you'll do a lot better than achieving a low goal.

What type of goals? Consider these:

1. *Applications.* Determine to write at least 10 applications a month. To achieve success, it's important to be an app writer. This point is well-covered elsewhere in this book. Set an application goal each month and fulfill that goal, even if the first app you write in a month is for a million dollars of face amount. Don't relax—accomplish your goal each month.

2. *Premium.* In addition, set a premium goal each month. As important as apps are, premium is pretty much what influences your commission payments. Determine what you need—and want—each month in the way of commissions and set the appropriate premium goal. I suggest something like $5,000 a month of premiums (1980 standards). Then increase your monthly premium goal each year. Don't relax until you achieve both the application and premium goal every month.

3. *MDRT membership.* Another must, another stepping stone. Achieving the above goals will guarantee MDRT membership every year.

Community Activity

Become involved in your community. Every community needs the services of people like you and me. Life insurance agents are especially valuable because they are, in a sense, self-employed and have more control of their schedules than those who work on a nine-to-five basis. Also, insurance salespeople tend to be motivated, energetic, and articulate, and these attributes lend themselves admirably to community work.

It's good to do something for your community, church or temple, and school system. One caution: don't become over-involved. Pick one area that fits your talents and available time. Then do the best job you can. Attitude is important: the reason you do community work is to perform valuable services for the people with whom you live. The work is not done to produce life insurance sales. If you do a creditable job, the sales may eventually follow. But it is unwise to enter this area with a design to directly increase your life insurance production.

Can you spare the time spent on community activities? Yes, you can. Consider it as an investment in your town and in your future. Your good works will mark you as the type of person with whom people will want to do business. It will show that you are willing to "pay back" what your community has given to you. America thrives because of the spirit of its citizens, their generosity, and their willingness to contribute.

At this point in my life, I find that I can give even more time than before to community activities. Yet my sales continue at a respectable rate. Organization is the key.

Relax

Take time to relax. No one can work 24 hours a day, seven days a week. No one can work simply for the financial rewards. As you know by now, the life insurance business is a demanding one, a stressful one, a pressure cooker. It is also a lonely business at times, and the world in which we operate can sometimes seem hostile, negative, and rejecting. Someone once called this business the highest paid hard work. Part of our compensation is the time and ability to relax and unwind.

You *must* stop every now and then and get away from the business for an hour, a day, a week, or a month. If you have earned the right to do so, don't deny yourself that right. I enjoy golfing. I love to fish. These things let me relax and unwind. My mind recharges, my body loosens up.

After the appropriate amount of relaxation, I find myself refreshed and eager to return to the challenges of selling. The juices start flowing again. It feels good to get back to the old routine. Work is important. Relaxation is, too. You have to strike the proper balance. Too much of either one is destructive.

Success is an important goal, especially for the newer agent. There is so much to learn at the start (and through the ensuing years), and seemingly so little time in which to learn it. There's only one person who can make you succeed—and that's you. Only *you* can work hard, and only *you* can keep going when the going is difficult. Only *you* can put in the hours and mental energy for CLU study and subsequent advanced training. Only *you* can choose appropriate goals and then fulfill them. All the managers and spouses in the world can only encourage you. Not one of them can make you do it. The "want" must come from within. Without self-motivation, nothing will be accomplished.

My Way

While going through life, particularly in my 20s and 30s, I experienced some setbacks. Perhaps these would not seem like setbacks to others, because I have never experienced a really bad year in the life insurance business. By setbacks I mean not always reaching the goals I was striving for. And to me, that is always a setback. But I believe those experiences caused me to become a stronger person. I learned to come to grips with myself. I learned to recognize the mistakes of my life and, from them, to see them in other peoples' lives and businesses. I learned what not to do in order to be successful.

11.

SOME THOUGHTS ON SECRETARIES AND OFFICE OPERATIONS

I owe a good deal of my success to a simple philosophy. If you can follow this simple rule, I believe that your sales results can be greatly improved—and your business life will become a lot more satisfying. My philosophy is this: Anything that doesn't call for my talents as a life insurance salesperson and that someone else can do, I should not do.

My secretaries help me put this into practice every day. For some years now, I have had two full-time secretaries. One young woman acts as my receptionist, greeting the public at my office and on the telephone. She makes appointments for me and answers calls to my office. She does my personal bookkeeping, takes care of business check writing, sees that all bills are paid, records ledger commission credits and makes sure that proper commissions have been paid to me, files a monthly report for my CPA and provides me with a quarterly report on such activities.

My second secretary is responsible for preparing illustrations, typing letters, getting the mail, answering it, and placing on my desk material that *I need to see.* Both secretaries are tuned-in to my philosophy and know that I don't want to have something come to my desk that they could have—or should have—done.

Thus, when the phone rings, I do not answer it. A competent individual takes care of the person calling—many times much better than I could have done. Most telephone calls to the office of any insurance agent do not require the personal attention of the agent. When your secretary handles your calls, you get two important benefits: First, you're provided with valuable minutes—which add up to hours each week—to do things only you can do. Second, your train of thought is not interrupted. You can concentrate on the task at hand, giving it 100 percent of your concentration.

Tangible Benefits

The business side of any agent's operation is extremely important and cannot be overlooked. But if an agent takes care of the hundreds of details, he or she doesn't get one dime extra in commissions and loses the time to make more sales. The correct approach is to have your secretary do what has to be done—*all* that has to be done. Every hour that I spend writing checks to pay bills or checking my ledger to insure that all commissions due me are paid is money lost to me. This is why a competent secretary is so necessary to me—and to you.

Twenty two years ago, I selected my first secretary and trained her. That was the last time I trained a secretary, since I always have my present secretaries train the new secretary who is coming to work for us. *It is too expensive for me to try to train each secretary.* My present staff knows exactly what I want, and they are in the best position to train someone new in the office.

At times, there are things that come up in the insurance business that a secretary will not know how to do. But that's not unique to this business. If something comes up that's "new," I know my secretaries will learn how to do it. Yes, mistakes may be made at first, but people learn from mistakes and the job gets done.

I have one secretary in charge of the office operation, and she reports to me. As a result, I have only one person to supervise. She acts as my office manager, and I lean heavily on her for all the minute details that go into the making of a successful life insurance sales operation. She's the first one who comes into the office in the morning. At times, she's the one who remains after hours if details are not complete.

A Typical Day

A typical day in my office begins shortly before 8:00 A.M. By that time, I've made some telephone contacts (the day starts early in Iowa) either from my home or from my car prior to arriving at the office. The first hour-and-a-half is spent in the office taking care of dictation and mail from the previous day—possibly preparing for an interview that is coming up.

My secretary generally arranges my first interview no later than 9:30 in the morning. I often try to have a luncheon appointment, and I try to have my secretary arrange another interview in the afternoon, hopefully at 1:30. This permits me to return to my office (if the appointment takes place out of my office) by 3:30. I then have time to put some finishing touches on work my staff has prepared for me, and it permits me to gear up for the next day. I'll frequently dictate into a recording machine, and one secretary will transcribe that the following morning.

My office operates *six days a week.* The secretaries "straddle" their hours so that one comes in a little before 8:00 A.M. and leaves around 4:30 P.M. The other one comes in at 8:30 and remains until 5. Since they take different lunch hours, the office remains open from 8 to 5, six days a week. The community and my clients know this, and people are pleased that they can obtain answers to their questions virtually whenever they want.

I like to keep in touch with my office during the day. Using my car radio-telephone, I call the office before I leave the car and let my staff know where I am, whom I'm seeing, and whether or not I should be contacted during the interview. As soon as I get out of the interview, I call in again, take any messages, and follow through with calls that I can return from the car.

As you can see, the car telephone is an important sales tool. With it, I am never out of contact with my office for more than two hours. If a prospect or client wishes to talk directly with me, the telephone permits this communication no matter where I am. And combining driving with talking is a good time-saver.

I prefer to have most of my interviews in my office. Many of these interviews are arranged by my secretaries. Having the secretary secure the interview in most cases is a natural outgrowth of the type of work I do.

At times, clients will tell me that they want to see me at least once a year. Their names go into our tickler file and, at the appropriate time, my secretary calls to make the desired appointment. These appointments are not hard to make, and experience proves that they can be made by my secretary.

Her appointment-making skill extends to calling clients to suggest an appointment to update an estate plan or to provide an annual update on the insurance policies. She also calls prospects as a follow-up to mailings we make of a four-page monthly information newsletter. She asks if they appreciate the material the newsletter contains, whether they read it, and whether they would like to continue receiving it. She also seeks to set up an appointment so that I can demonstrate my services.

She has heard me often enough on the telephone and has adopted virtually the same language that I use. She indicates to the prospect or client that I'm out of the office and that she is calling to see if she can arrange a time that would be agreeable to both the prospect and to me to discuss an update of an estate plan, a review of policies, or whatever.

She says something like this:

"Mr. Prospect, this is _______, secretary of Don Van Der Weide of New York Life Insurance Company. He was referred to you by one of his clients who is a friend of yours (mentions name). Don has been doing some estate planning work for (client) and he seems very pleased with Don's work. Don asked him if he knew someone who would appreciate the type of work Don does, and he mentioned your name. The reason that I'm calling is to see if we can arrange a mutually convenient time for Don to show you the type of work he does."

Our experience has shown that we have had good success with my secretary making the call since the prospect or client knows that he or she is not talking to the person who is trying to get the interview. The prospect knows that he or she can say no to the secretary very easily. But then she'll come back and say: "Well, you know that you really have nothing to lose. Perhaps it might be taxes saved and money in your pocket if you will take a few moments out of your busy schedule to see if you can keep together all that you have worked so hard for all your life."

Perhaps your secretary does the same thing for you. If not, why not try having your secretary make these appointment calls. It saves your time, it's prestigious when the secretary does it well, and —it works!

Compensation

My secretaries do a good job, and they are important to my success. Each is paid a good salary, and each gets bonuses. I like to give bonuses at least *six* times a year. By doing this, I feel that I can properly repay the office staff for the work they are doing and also provide them with earnings beyond what I might normally pay if I had them on a flat monthly salary. In addition, I provide fringe benefits such as group life insurance and group health insurance for their families.

My office operation is tremendously important to me. I must be able to exercise my sales skills and talents. In my operation, I'm the only one who can secure the dollars which pay for the salaries, the rent, the utilities, and the equipment. To sell effectively, my mind must be free of details which directly contribute nothing to producing sales. A trained, smooth-functioning office is, therefore, a must.

If you're relatively new to life insurance sales, you may not have a secretary yet. I suggest that you hire one, even if you have to start with a part-time worker. You can't afford to be without a secretary. When you do hire a secretary, have this person relieve you of everything that you should not be doing. You're paid to sell life insurance; your secretary is paid to help you do just that.

If you already have a secretary, I suggest that you explore even more ways she or he can aid you. Remember my philosophy: Anything that doesn't utilize my sales skills and talents and that someone else can do, I should not do. Not only does this make me a more powerful salesperson, it does wonders for my secretary. It elevates her from the ranks of a clerk-typist and recognizes her as an intelligent individual who is charged with the responsibility of running the inside of a life insurance sales organization. The better she does her job, the better the organization will run. I can attest to that.

My Way

We must measure our performance. Is it up to the standard that we would set for others in a similar position? We must keep up with changing times. We should know what we want and be sure that we have the real desire to progress through constant growth. You and I cannot become successful agents just because we like the idea. We need to develop the desire by studying and practicing so as to learn to deal not only with everyday routine affairs, but also with complex situations that occasionally arise. We need to be problem solvers. When we approach prospects on what they want for their families, we soon find we are talking about the same thing. Not life insurance but the benefits of life insurance. Since we are offering them something they already want, it shouldn't be hard to make them want it enough to part with the premium.

12.

HOW I PROMOTE SALES

Sales promotion is important to me. No matter how many years you have been in the business, no matter how many clients you have, you must constantly be looking for tomorrow's prospects with an eye to making sales to them.

An important part of my sales promotion is a monthly newsletter called *Planned Financial Security,* prepared exclusively for my company's agents by Farnsworth Publishing Company. The newsletter is a personalized four page, 8½ x 11 affair, written for the "typical" prospect in a clear, simple manner. This newsletter performs a number of functions for me.

First, it keeps my name in front of my AAA clients and prospects. It's a reminder of my interest in them and their financial problems, as well as my desire to serve them. At least once a month, these people think of Don Van Der Weide.

Second, it's a way for me to sow ideas. Some of the content of *Planned Financial Security* describes applications of life insurance to problems faced by estate owners, business executives, and heads of families. The style of the newsletter gets the reader involved in the message and, in many cases, the reader sees a problem which he or she faces, along with a suggested solution.

For example, the owner of a minority interest in a close corporation sees the problem his heirs will face when he dies. It's all described in a story in the newsletter, and a suggestion or two for overcoming the problem is offered. There's no hard sell, no pushing of life insurance. But the message gets across to the reader. Often I'll get a call from a client or prospect who wants more information about something mentioned in *Planned Financial Security.* I can directly trace a number of sales to my mailing of this valuable sales promotion piece.

How many times have you felt that if you could just get a chance to tell your story to a prospect, he or she would see the logic of your viewpoint and the need for life insurance? Many people won't let you tell your story verbally—at least not on your initial approach—and thus the newsletter format is a good way to reach such hard-to-see prospects. After mailing the newsletter for a number of months you can pick up the phone, call the prospect, and suggest a follow-up based on some of the ideas that have been published in your newsletter.

Every person who comes into my office in town is welcome to take—free of charge—a cap bearing my company's logo. You've seen caps like these worn by hundreds of people. They're good-looking and comparable to those sold in golf pro shops. They're fun to wear, and they add a jaunty touch to any casual outfit.

There's a box of these caps on the counter in my office. I also keep a supply in my car's trunk and at home.

If someone drops in, he or she can take a cap. Many do so and wear them. I buy the caps in large quantities and can afford to give them away. When my prospects wear these caps, they're endorsing my company—and me. The caps have led to some interesting sales.

For example, I had given a cap to a client who is also a salesman (of products for farmers). He was wearing the cap one day as he made a sales call on a farmer. During the discussion, the farmer, who had noticed the cap, asked my client where he could contact a New York Life agent.

My client said that he thought Don Van Der Weide would be the person to talk to. The salesman returned to town, called me, and suggested that I give the farmer a call. I followed through and subsequently sold $200,000 of Whole Life to the farmer and his wife, basing the sale on an estate conservation need—and more life insurance will come on the sons who are farming with their father.

Here was a prospect who lived 60 miles away from my home. I had never heard of him and he had never heard of me. He was interested in estate planning and had been told by his lawyer that he should purchase some insurance to cover final costs. Seeing the logo on the cap worn by my client had made him ask where he might reach an insurance agent. It belabors the obvious for me to say that if the cap hadn't been worn, I would have missed a sale—a substantial one—which paid for many, many caps.

Guaranteed Insurability Options

Page 111 shows a copy of the letter my secretary prepares for my signature. It's sent to every client who has a guaranteed insurability option rider (my company calls it the Policy Purchase Option). At this point, let me strongly endorse the addition of such an option to every policy you sell.

I find this option offers two strong advantages to me as a salesman:

1. It gives me the ability to guarantee that the client can buy more insurance at specified times in the future. Neither of us has to worry about a rating or declination. The insurance, at standard rates, is guaranteed.

2. It gives me a reason to call the client, if no other opportunity to do so presents itself. The options to buy come up every three years or when the insured (or spouse) has a child born or adopted. My call invariably leads to a re-evaluation of insurance needs, with the chances of a new sale rather promising. If the client is still a standard risk, the sale is generally considerably more than the amount guaranteed under the option. If he or she is not a standard risk, the guaranteed amount is a good start—at standard rates—on the additional insurance he or she needs.

If you add the guaranteed insurability option to every eligible policy you write, and if you use a letter like the one I send, all that you need is a simple "tickler" file to provide the name of the insured a month or so before the option date occurs. You and your secretary can devise a 3 x 5 index card system, arranged by months and years, so that the client's card automatically presents itself at the proper time. Once noted, it is refiled to appear at the next appropriate time.

The Policy Purchase Option has produced an amazing amount of business for me. It can do the same for you.

Age Changes

Age changes are akin to guaranteed insurability. An age change presents an opportunity to call on the client and to offer something of value. The letter on page 112 is prepared by my secretary for my signature, and we send it out a few weeks before the insurance age change takes place.

Don't overlook this basic sales promotion idea; it's produced millions of dollars of business for me.

Other Ideas

When something noteworthy happens to a prospect or client, I drop him or her a note, complimenting the achievement. My wife and my secretaries have sharp eyes and check the local newspapers, etc., for these items which are so important to the individual. Chances are my note is the only written acknowledgement received by the person, and it is greatly appreciated.

Birthday cards fall into this category. When you leave your childhood, hardly anyone sends you a birthday card. Perhaps this is why an insurance agent's card is appreciated. The cost is incidental, but the results are long-lasting.

I use roadside signs. They have impact. As my clients and prospects drive around Orange City, my name and company identification on a sign remind them that I'm available to be of service to the community.

Finally, I use ads on local radio and television stations. The cost of these isn't great, and they're a good way of keeping my name in front of the public.

Sales promotion has to be an ongoing, continuous program of keeping you in front of your public. Its cost is just another business investment, one guaranteed to repay you many times.

Back to Case Rate

Before I end this chapter on sales promotion, let me again mention case rate. As I've already noted, success for me has come from the number of applications I write. I have more places to go, more people to see, and more chances to plant seeds. Planting seeds is another form of sales promotion for me. Because I planted a lot of seeds years ago, some of them—especially during the past few years—have sprouted into good sales, real gems. And I didn't have just one or two new gems, there were a lot of them.

Most of my business is repeat business. Normally, 80 percent of my sales come from repeat business. In this past year, however, I had fewer repeat sales than I had for the prior three years. To compensate, I did a lot of joint field work with other agents. I guess my reputation is a form of sales promotion for me. As I achieved my goals, other agents seemed to acquire increased confidence in me and called on me to join with them in closing cases. They built third-party influence for me with their clients, and the interviews—and closes—went well.

My Way

I have the ability to give a listening ear to problems and objectives. I am a good listener. I have the prospect's best interests at heart. This is better than overpowering him with language and sections of the code. I boil down his objections into two or three sentences he can understand. This is true whether I am talking to the prospect, his attorney, or his accountant. If we are not in agreement, then all may be useless since we're not doing what the prospect wants done.

Policy Purchase Option Letter

Just a short note to let you know that you have an option available at this time to purchase an additional $________ of Whole Life insurance without evidence of insurability at your insurance age of________. I strongly recommend that you take advantage of this option at your present age since your premium rate will be lower, and your dividend and retirement values will be higher.

Should you desire more information about this option available to you, please give me a call and we can set up an appointment to discuss this further.

May I please hear from you?

Respectfully yours,

Age Change Letter

We would like to save you money in your future insurance purchases. You are aware, I'm sure, that as you get older you have to pay a higher rate on any new insurance policies you buy. Perhaps you are not aware though that the rate change goes into effect six months before your birthday.

Since you probably expect to buy more insurance some day, perhaps you should consider it before ________in order to take advantage of the lower premium rate.

I plan to call you before this date to give you any information you might like to have.

I hope this new year brings you health, happiness, and prosperity.

Respectfully yours,

DON VAN DER WEIDE, CLU
Sales Representative

13.

STUDY GROUPS CAN BE VALUABLE

I guess just about every life insurance agent goes through some type of "basic training" in securing a state license and in learning something about product and needs for insurance. Then a good number go through a company training program to gain more knowledge and skills. Some get involved with LUTC, and some even go on to CLU. Although the life insurance industry, through its companies and associations, offers a variety of technical and skill training, many agents just stop studying at some point. It's natural when you've been in the business for a number of years and are successful at what you're doing to play down the importance of continued training. Because of this, study groups are an excellent way to keep up with changing developments and to enhance your sales skills even further.

What It Is

A study group is just that: a group of life insurance agents who meet from time to time to study together. It's a way to learn from the very best teachers—other agents. Life insurance salespeople tend to learn best from other insurance salespeople, probably because of a tendency to accept what is offered by one's peers. You trust them and have confidence in their abilities. If it works for them, why shouldn't it work for you?

A study group can be an exciting stimulant for the person who sells life insurance. No one knows better than you that this is a lonely business, one built on achieving success in spite of daily rejection. Your sales stimulate you, yes, but what strength you can draw from your fellow agents, especially the ones you admire and respect.

How It Started

I have belonged to a study group for 10 years. With few exceptions, the group has consisted of the same people, a cross-section of the agents representing my company. They come from different states, work in different markets, and have been in the insurance business for varying numbers of years. We formed the group at a company convention. There was a common bond of respect, affection, and desire to do something tangible to make ourselves more successful as individuals. Although we had a pretty good opinion of our abilities as insurance salespersons, we knew that there was much more to learn in many areas besides selling, although sales skills certainly would not be overlooked in our deliberations.

We meet two times a year. One meeting takes place at our company's Chairmans Council convention, which is a five-day educational conference in itself. The other meeting takes four days, and we meet in such places as Texas, Arizona, and Hawaii, enjoying the fringe benefit of sunshine when much of the nation is still knee-deep in winter.

Ah, you say, a junket to warmer climes under the guise of a study group. What a wonderful idea! Although our meeting spot is a pleasant one, most of our hours are spent hard at work. Let me tell you how the study group works.

How It Works

First, we have a formal agenda. There's no sitting around a room, casually chatting about "what's new?" Before we meet, we all agree on the major topics to be discussed. We share input through correspondence and telephone calls, pooling our thoughts and feelings. Where do we feel the need for information? What new developments in the industry seem to be worth in-depth exploration by the group? "What's new" may be one of our interests, but by the time it arrives ready for the study group, it is a well thought-out, well-planned approach.

Our next step is to choose a chairman. He is selected each year on a rotating basis, and he is the boss of the meeting's preparation. When our discussion topics have been determined, it's up to the chairman to assign topics to specific members. In this process, he uses his good judgment and his knowledge of the talents, abilities, and operating procedures of the respective members of the group. In this way, he blocks in the hours that will fill up (literally!) our four days of meetings.

Once a member has been assigned a topic, he begins to work on a presentation that he will make on the subject at our meeting. The presentation, including question-and-answer repartee, will last several hours. The member, knowing that he will be expected to answer each and every question on the topic posed by fellow members, devotes numerous hours to his presentation preparation. I know that I have spent a tremendous amount of time on my presentations. We're all spending time and money being at the study group, and each member must receive a substantial dividend. Therefore, each presentation sparkles, revealing the effort placed into it.

What do we talk about? Obviously, one of our topics is sales ideas, but the general area of sales is not that important to us. Each member is successful and isn't desperate for a hot sales idea. Of course, in-depth presentations of successful, proven ideas are not disregarded. But a good amount of our time is spent on matters important to us as business executives.

This is where the study group has particular value, especially to me. I'm not looking for sales ideas; I have a good number of them. I know what works well for me in my market, and I don't have to constantly seek "new" ideas to dangle in front of my prospects. My methods are pretty much meat-and-potato approaches, and they have given me and my family a good standard of living. Where I want to learn more and to improve myself is in the area of operating my business. I believe that other members of the study group feel this way, too.

So we'll spend hours on the discussion of operating an office. How do you make the decision of where to operate from? Should you work out of the company's main office in your area, or should you open your own office in a different building or locality? Should you operate an office at home? What are the relative advantages or disadvantages? What are the respective costs? What are the tax write-offs?

A member's presentation serves as a springboard for a discussion where each member gets many opportunities to say, "I think," "I feel," "The way I do it is . . .," and so forth. Although I operate my own office in Orange City, I can learn a lot from the agent who has a suite of offices in the company's main office. We get into many other topics of interest to us as businesspersons. How do you train a secretary? What standards do you set up to measure secretarial performance? When you have a good secretary, how do you compensate this person in order to keep her or him? What fringe benefits are available? As I said, I feel pretty confident in approaching people about life insurance and selling a good amount of it. But when I first hired a secretary—and then additional help—I was in uncharted waters. I wanted to be fair and to compensate my staff for performance, and I needed more direction in this regard.

The group helped me as a businessman by furnishing ideas based on practical experience. As I listened to and participated in the discussions, I had a chance to make mental and written notes. That idea sounded good. I don't think I could use that one, though. Say, there's a thought—let me probe that one a little deeper. And so it went. A study group leads to many heady discussions.

The group has helped me become a better salesman, too. One member will have an excellent telephone approach, or the way he says something might be just what I need to overcome an objection I have been encountering. Another member might have an excellent letter on term conversion, something that I could use to make a few more permanent insurance sales each and every year. Another might offer an approach for selling insurance under a guaranteed insurability option. Still another might have something that my secretary could do to ease the way for more sales for me.

By now you know that the members of our study group are not only capable, they're generous. This is a prime requirement for each member. He or she must be unselfish—a giver. The only way to increase your individual storehouse of ideas is to receive from one another. With ideas, you never lose what you give away. In fact, as you offer the idea, another may make it even better, and now you have an even more valuable and useful idea.

We don't have any conversation controllers in our group. The interchange of ideas is give and take, with no one individual dominating the discussion. Everyone gets his chance to take the floor and express his thoughts, and participation is pretty even. There is no final word on any topic. Each member says what he thinks, based on his own experience. With a chairperson, an agenda, and assigned presentation givers, the hours move right along and the ideas flow almost endlessly.

Starting Your Own Group

That's how our study group works. If you belong to such a group, you might be able to pick up an idea or two from our group. I hope so. If you're not a member of a study group and the above discussion has stimulated your thinking along those lines, let me offer a few tips on forming such a group.

1. Since you're starting from scratch, mentally determine which of your associates might be willing to join a study group. Pick out ones who are successful career agents, people that you feel have a lot to offer. Think of the ones who are givers, the ones who seem to give of their time and talents to various industry, business, and charitable activities.

2. Discuss the concept of a study group with them individually. If there seems to be an interest, arrange a meeting and talk out the matter. Is there genuine interest? Are the members compatable? Is there mutual respect for the abilities of others? Will each one be able to give of his or her time to act as rotating chairman,

presentation giver, and contributor of ideas? Is each unselfish, a giver? Will each be able to take several days out of the work schedule to meet as a group, probably in a location away from your home town? And, most important, is the chemistry of the group such that a valuable and honest interchange of ideas will take place?

3. Assuming that a study group looks feasible, have the members pick subjects to explore over a day or two. Elect a chairperson and select members to prepare presentations. Pick a tentative date and place to meet. Then see what transpires. Did the chairperson do the job? Did the presentation-givers work at it? Did the meeting take place? How was the discussion? Evaluate all the components. Was the meeting of the group worthwhile? Did each member participate? Did each member get something of value? Should you do it again?

A study group can be a waste of time for some agents. Some may think of the meeting as a wonderful vacation, a chance to sit around the pool, sipping cool drinks and swapping yarns. For these agents, a study group will not be valuable. But for those agents who consider it as an educational conference, an interchange of ideas between capable peers, the group could pay handsome dividends. It has done so for me over the past 10 years. My business has improved. I have formed deeper friendships with my friends in the group. And I feel I am making better use of my abilities and the time I have in which to work.

My Way

There was a prospect, a person I had worked with several years ago. He was a successful and dynamic person, but like so many, negligent in his financial affairs. He needed more life insurance and a new will, and he knew it. But he didn't feel the urgency and I failed to make him feel it. He died last year. I was determined that this wouldn't happen again. I explained what happened to his family and business associates. The circumstances were clear and achingly relevant. The value of life insurance—what it can mean in estate conservation and in peace of mind—was now too obvious to ignore. The survivors could apply it to their own situation and were motivated to see that the mistake would not be repeated. And as I worked for them in this vital area, the realization of the profound effect we can have on people's lives came to me. I pray I never lose it.

14.

THE INSURANCE YOU YOURSELF OWN

There's a relationship between what an agent owns and what he or she sells.

Every successful agent I know owns a substantial amount of life insurance, and this ownership reflects a belief in the product which carries over into the agent's sales activity. The more you own, the more you'll sell.

Let me give you a rule of thumb which is borne out by the experience of the top life insurance producers I know: You will sell an amount of life insurance in a month equal to what you personally own.

That's an exciting concept, isn't it?

Do you want to sell more life insurance? The answer is deceptively simple. *Own* more.

Do you want to *sell* a million a month? *Own* a million dollars of life insurance. If these figures seem somewhat heady for a newcomer, how about sales of $2.5 million a year? Simply own $200,000 of insurance.

It's amazing how strong this ownership can make you in selling. When the prospect indicates that he or she is insurance poor or can't afford it, you can simply nod in agreement and say that you sometimes have the same feelings about the life insurance you own. And then you go into a brief discussion of why you own the amount of life insurance you do own, possibly even mentioning the amount you have in force. This gets the discussion back on the right track, the *need* for insurance, not the *cost* of the insurance.

Capital Need Analysis

I prefer the Capital Need Analysis approach. Simply stated, this calls for a capital sum (provided by life insurance) which, at an assumed rate of interest, will provide the income needed by the family. For example, if the family needs $20,000 a year and 10 percent yield is realistic, then $200,000 of life insurance proceeds would be required under the Capital Need approach. As you can realize, this conserves the principal amount, with the family living on income from the invested sum.

This approach is easily understood by the average prospect, and it permits the prospect to choose an interest rate which he or she feels is realistic. It has the added advantage of conservation of principal which is one less objection to face in the closing inverview.

With the Capital Need Analysis, I use trusts, too, as I have indicated throughout the text of this book.

I've used two types of trusts: a marital deduction type of trust, and a trust in Eunice's will. Eleven years ago, I began using a Clifford type of trust with the children as income beneficiaries. I won't go into the details of these trusts except to note that when an agent uses trusts in his or her personal estate planning, it's easier to explain them to a prospect. You can certainly speak with more conviction when recommending their use.

An additional—and important—benefit is that, in order to get such instruments drafted for your own use, you will seek out an attorney who is skilled in this area, and the professional relationship that can come from this can be of great use to you in your sales activity.

The Irrevocable Life Insurance Trust

As you've noted, I'm high on the use of the irrevocable life insurance trust. It has a number of advantages:

- The proceeds of the policy are not includable in the donor's estate if he or she lives three years after the policy has transferred to the trust.

- Use of the trust can help to avoid estate taxation at the subsequent death of the spouse.

- The trustee can be given some discretion to make loans to the estate or to purchase assets from it to provide liquidity.

- The trustee will manage the property of the trust under terms set down by the creator of the trust.

- The assets of the trust will not be subject to claims by creditors of the insured or his or her spouse.

- Because of the discretion given to the trustee, provisions can be made for the unforseen needs of the beneficiary.

- Through the medium of the trust, ownership problems that would otherwise arise if divorce occurs can be avoided.

• The ultimate beneficiaries of the trust corpus can still be chosen by the grantor and included in the trust instrument.

•The delays and expenses connected with probate can be avoided. Trust property doesn't pass through the probate process.

• If the trust is well-designed, the creator can get a federal income tax deduction for interest paid by the trustee on a policy loan.

Of course, as in any arrangement, there is a trade-off of some advantages. For example:

• When an in-force policy is transferred to the trust, the owner suffers loss of ownership.

• Such a transfer could result in a gift tax situation.

• If the donor needs the property transferred to the trust in the future, it's beyond his or her control. Therefore, before any transactions are made, they have to be well thought-out.

The use of irrevocable life insurance trusts can lead to the sale of substantial amounts of life insurance since many estate owners are looking for methods of avoiding inclusion of insurance proceeds in their estates and are looking for liquidity in both the husband's and wife's estate without the proceeds being includable.

Twenty-five percent of the insurance I sell is in connection with such a trust. I explain the trust workings on a yellow pad of paper. With it, I illustrate what happens when the estate owner places property in the trust, and what happens after death when the insurance proceeds flow into the trust. The final "illustration" is a series of lines, words, and arrows (denoting flow of dollars), but it gets the point across to the prospect. Of course, I work closely with an attorney in the creation of the trust.

My Way

My wife, Eunice, recently cut out a brief article from the newspaper for me. It contained some remarks by the noted religious author, Neil Strait. I was particularly struck by this observation:

> *The greatest task a person can engage in is the task of serving others. For in that endeavor, he is not only helping others, he is bettering himself. Something grows taller in a person when he reaches out to others.*

I have never seen the idea of service put in quite those terms before. Yet, it does explain that feeling we get inside when we've helped someone. It explains the sense of accomplishment that comes not from merely doing a job well, but from doing an important job well, a job that has left someone else better off, more secure, and reasonably at peace in a risky world.

15.

THE INSURANCE THAT EVENTUALLY PAYS FOR ITSELF

The "Premium Offset Plan" has received a lot of publicity in recent years. It is an interesting concept to the insurance salesperson, and it is an intriguing idea to the person who pays for the life insurance. With Premium Offset, the policyowner can be freed from making premium payments on a life insurance policy after a number of years, usually long before the end of the normal premium payment period. Who wouldn't be interested in a plan which lets you stop making premium payments on a policy "out of pocket" after, say, 12 years, instead of having to pay premiums for the rest of the policyowner's life?

I've used Premium Offset for many years, long before computerized illustrations specifically designed for it were available. I never offer it as an idea in itself. Instead, I make it part of a discussion with the prospect concerning how the life insurance proposed can be paid for. I like to put my packages together to assure my prospect the he or she is, in a sense, able to have his or her cake and eat it, too.

If you haven't heard of Premium Offset, let me explain it for you. Premium Offset is the name given to this concept by New York Life. Your company may have a different term for it. Read the explanation given to this plan in this chapter and see if your company offers illustrations on the plan. If you have heard of it and know how it works, let me explain why it's valuable for both you and your client. Premium Offset will help you to close many more sales if you approach your prospects correctly.

What It Is

Premium Offset is an excellent way to illustrate the dividend addition option that is found in a participating life insurance policy. This option permits the insured to buy additional paid-up insurance in lieu of the cash dividend he or she would be entitled to. Since each piece of paid-up insurance is, in effect, a separate "policy," it has a cash value of its own which grows year by year, and it's eligible for dividends separate from the dividends paid by the basic policy. If your company offers participating policies and they contain the dividend addition option, you can offer the premium offset plan to your clients and prospects. If your company provides you with computerized illustrations on Premium Offset, your explaining—and selling—job will be that much easier.

Speaking of computerized illustrations, on pages 130 and 131 is a computerized illustration prepared by my company which illustrates a $100,000 Whole Life policy issued to a male, age 35. The annual premium is $1,913.

In reviewing the illustration, you'll note that the face amount of the dividend additions and the cash value of the dividend additions grow year after year. For the first 13 years, this illustration is no different from any other dividend addition statement. But at the end of the 13th year, the magic of the Premium Offset plan takes effect.

The premium is still $1,913, and the face amount of the policy is still $100,000. The face amount of the dividend additions is $10,947, and the cash value of these additions is $6,556. We now come to the 14th year.

Instead of paying the $1,913 out of pocket, the insured lets Premium Offset take over. He or she takes the cash dividend paid at the end of the 13th year and then dips into the dividend account and uses whatever is necessary to pay the rest of the premium which is not covered by the the 13th year dividend.

After this simple transaction, here is what will happen:

1. The Premium for the 14th year has been paid. Therefore, the policy continues in force.

2. The cash value of the dividend additions increases through the year because of interest.

3. The basic policy earns a dividend at the end of the 14th year.

4. The paid-up additions earn a dividend at the end of the 14th year.

The 15th year comes up, and the process is repeated.

The insured takes the cash dividend payable at the end of the 14th year and then dips into the dividend account for the remainder of the premium. After this has been done, the policy and dividend value again increase. As the illustration shows, the insured will never have to pay a premium out-of-pocket again, assuming dividends are earned as illustrated.

PREMIUM OFFSET PROPOSAL
SURRENDERING PAID-UP ADDITIONS TO PAY PREMIUMS IN LATER YEARS.

PREPARED FOR — PRESENTED BY AGENT

AGE 35M

PLAN - $100,000 WHOLE LIFE

	YEARLY ILLUSTRATION			CUMULATIVE ILLUSTRATION			
YEAR	BASIC PREMIUM OUTLAY	INCREASE IN TOTAL CASH VALUE*++	DIFFERENCE + OR– *++	GUARANTEED CASH VALUE	CASH VALUE OF PAID-UP ADDNS*	TOTAL CASH VALUE *++	DEATH BENEFIT BEG. YR. *++
1	$1,913		$1,913–				$100,000
2	1,913	$1,462	451–	$1,400	$62	$1,462	100,000
3	1,913	1,920	7+	3,200	182	3,382	100,178
4	1,913	1,983	70+	5,000	364	5,364	100,502
5	1,913	2,081	168+	6,800	646	7,446	100,974
6	1,913	2,267	354+	8,700	1,013	9,713	101,669
7	1,913	2,454	541+	10,700	1,466	12,166	102,527
8	1,913	2,448	535+	12,600	2,014	14,614	103,542
9	1,913	2,747	834+	14,700	2,661	17,361	104,705
10	1,913	2,854	941+	16,800	3,415	20,215	106,009

11	1,913	2,790	877+	18,700	4,305	23,005	107,458
12	1,913	3,047	1,134+	20,700	5,352	26,052	109,103
13	1,913	3,204	1,291+	22,700	6,556	29,256	110,947
(A) 14		1,959	1,959+	24,800	5,915	31,215	109,201
15		1,725	1,725+	26,900	5,340	32,940	108,177
16		1,902	1,902+	29,100	4,842	34,842	107,064
17		1,978	1,978+	31,300	4,420	36,820	106,165
18		2,266	2,266+	33,600	4,086	39,086	105,464
19		2,357	2,357+	35,900	3,843	41,443	105,063
20		2,558	2,558+	38,300	3,701	44,001	104,852
(B) 20		2,558	2,558+	38,300	3,701	44,001	104,852
AT 60		2,775	2,775+	47,500	6,500	56,500	108,038
AT 65		3,196	3,196+	56,300	12,190	71,490	115,073
AT 70		3,647	3,647+	64,500	21,416	88,916	125,269

(A) First year that premiums are paid by surrendering paid-up additions.

(B) Year in which dividend values reach their lowest point after offset year.

This illustration is based on the present illustrative dividend scale, under which the dividend values will cover all premium payments after the number of years indicated (except for premiums for any supplementary benefits or riders which may be retained). If dividends are reduced in some future years, the value of paid-up additions may not cover the basic annual premium as illustrated.

That is the Premium Offset Plan. Its mechanics are simple and easily explained to a prospective insured, especially when a computerized illustration provides the calculations for you. *The main thing that the prospect is interested in is at what point he or she can stop paying premiums out of pocket*, assuming that dividends will continue as illustrated. When Premium Offset shows that a 35-year-old need look forward to only 13 years of premiums on a whole life policy, you have extra sales power indeed.

Selling With Premium Offset

Before computerized illustrations made Premium Offset so easy to explain to a prospect, I didn't use a specific illustration. I simply explained to a prospect very carefully that past dividends and future dividends at a point in time would be adequate to pay subsequent premiums.

A lot of brilliant minds in the life insurance business have come up with novel ways to use Premium Offset. If you can master just one or two of these approaches, you can sell a lot of life insurance.

For example, consider combining the Premium Offset concept with the concept of discounting life insurance premiums. By discounting, I refer to the prepayment of life insurance premiums. The discount rate given today by most life insurance companies is attractive, adding to the effectiveness of an illustration combining Premium Offset and discounted premiums. Here's how it works:

We'll use an example of a male, age 0. Looking at a computerized illustration for this age, we note that the normal time required for payment of premiums under the Premium Offset Plan is 11 years—not a bad bargain in itself. But look what happens when you can *discount* those 11 years of premiums!

If a parent or grandparent wishes to make a single payment and repay the 11 years of premiums, only $5,863 will be required to give this young man $100,000 of insurance for the rest of his life. That's not a bad bargain, is it—$100,000 of insurance for an initial outlay of $5,863?

And here's more flexibility. If the $5,863 is a little too much for the parents to lay out, here's what they can pay per year if they wish to do it over several years:

Face Amount of Insurance Purchased (Male, Age 0)

Year	Two Payments	Three Payments	Four Payments	Six Payments
1	$3087	$1914	$1271	$1271
2	2949	2352	1929	1325
3		1960	1710	1247
4			1514	1174
5				1105
6				536
Totals	6036	6226	6424	6558

Of course, a package like this can be very attractive from a gift tax point of view since gifts of $3,000 can be made free of gift tax each year by one person to as many persons as the donor wishes. When husbands and wives join in making the gift, $6,000 can be given to any individual each year.

In this regard, look at the effect of the gift tax exemption when $3,000 or $6,000 is applied under the Premium Offset Plan over a number of years. These figures show how much life insurance can be purchased when the $3,000 or $6,000 amounts are applied at one time to buy a policy under the Premium Offset Plan.

Payment Amount	Single Payment	Two Payments	Three Payments	Four Payments	Six Payments
$3,000	$ 49,384	$ 97,082	$128,541	$157,485	$231,005
6,000	102,425	197,899	260,653	318,542	465,582

If you have a prospect who wants to do something for his or her children or grandchildren, don't overlook the sales power of the Premium Offset Plan.

Remember my earlier comment: I never offer Premium Offset as an idea in itself. You must sell a basic idea, a need for insurance. The value of Premium Offset lies in the reassurance the prospect receives concerning his or her ability to pay premiums in the future. With Premium Offset, the prospect need only look a relatively few years into the future. Whole life doesn't have to mean paying premiums for the rest of your life.

Note: The figures shown in this chapter which are based on dividends are for illustration purposes only. They are not a guarantee, promise, or estimate of any company's results. Use your own company's dividends for your illustrations.

16.

SELLING LIFE INSURANCE TO FARMERS

Much of my success in the life insurance business is due to selling to farmers. About one-third of my sales are made to farmers, so you can see a substantial amount of volume each year comes from this very good market.

The farm market today is tremendous, both in terms of numbers of farms and in their average size. Iowa, the state in which I live and work, has over 117,000 farms, with the average value being $188,000. Try to imagine the number of small businesses available to you for prospecting, especially since each one has a demonstrable need for life insurance.

Let's look at several other states to help convince you of the value of the farm market. According to recent statistics provided by the United States Department of

Agriculture, here is the average value of farms in such states as:

Colorado	$264,000
Florida	278,000
Montana	298,000
California	322,000

Even New Jersey, located in the heart of the northeast industrial complex, has almost 75,000 farms with an average value of $234,000!

The Modern Farm

These figures should help to dispel any outdated image one may have of the farmer. He may wear overalls and have mud on his shoes, but he is a modern businessperson in charge of a valuable business, valuable not only to the nation but to himself and to his family. The average farmer owns 400 acres of fruitful land, land which seems to be growing in value day by day, year by year.

The farmer uses modern equipment in the myriad of details around the farm: in planting, irrigating, fertilizing, and harvesting. Computer technology assists him in a myriad of tasks from taking care of his crops to preparing the payroll for the hired help. In short, the farmer is an experienced, college-educated, savvy individual—used to planning ahead and handling large sums of money. The modern farmer can write a check for a large premium as easily as he can write one for a new tractor—if he's convinced of the need for the purchase.

I enjoy working with farmers. They're independent, do their own thinking, their own thing, and are interesting and fun to work with. I approach them and talk to them as I do any successful businessperson on Main Street in my town. My prospects come from referred leads and from satisfied clients. At this point, you know how I work and how long I have worked in and around Orange City. Once I get the name of a farmer who may need my services, I have my secretary call on the telephone in order to arrange an appointment.

My interview procedure is basically the same as with any other family head, business executive, and estate owner. My sales talk is basically the same as I use with other prospects. It doesn't have to be different—the farmer has the same basic type of problem as anyone else. The assets may be different, but the problems are the same.

The Farm Estate

Let's consider a typical farmer and assume that he's age 45, married, has a son and daughter, and owns 500 acres. He works hard, earns a good income, and is pretty much in debt. Because of inflation, his spread grows in value each year. His farm represents his life's work, and he wants it to stay in the family. If he dies before retirement, he'd like the farm to pass to his son, with provision made for his widow, and with the daughter's welfare taken into account, too. Perhaps her future husband might help work the farm on a partnership basis with the son.

This farmer needs to make plans now to guarantee that his dreams will come true. He may think of himself as "wealthy," but the size of his farm estate, in addition to his personal assets, invaribly will present an estate tax problem. With some farm prospects, I find that my greatest service is to get them thinking about the financial planning problems they have. My next service is to get them to so something about the problems.

Cash is the most important item life insurance can provide to the farmer. With cash, his estate can pay all his debts and taxes. Cash can give the family time to get over the financial loss caused by the farmer's death, and it can hire people to do the tasks formerly done by the farmer. Cash can tide the family over until a son or son-in-law can run the farm. So, you see, I sell cash to the farmer, and I do it for pennies on the dollar each year.

What if the farmer's estate and family don't have cash at his death? How will they pay off debts, and how will they pay taxes? Without sufficient cash, they have only one recourse: to sell the farm, either entirely or in part. Since it may very well be a forced sale, the price they get for the farm or for individual acres may be much less than the true value. If all of the farm—or most of it—must be sold, the farmer, in effect, forces his family to leave its home and to foresake its livelihood. The farm that was to stay in the family becomes only a memory.

Life insurance simply provides cash to the family. Life insurance helps the family to keep the farm for future generations. Life insurance permits the family to stay in the home it has always loved and cherished and makes a promising future much more secure. In short, life insurance can make the farmer's plans and dreams come true.

The Farm Business

For a minute, forget the farmer as a person who manages the output of land and/or animals. Think of the farmer as a person in business, and in your mind go over the needs for business insurance with which you're familiar. Let's look at some analogies to illustrate how business life insurance applies to farmers.

There's the sole proprietor farmer. As noted above, he needs cash in his estate when he dies to be sure his family can continue the business. But he must make definite plans now to guarantee that his executor will be able to continue the farm business. A will giving the executor the authority to continue operation of the business is a must. In sales of this nature, you'll find that your conversation with the farmer *first* centers on the practical aspects of operation of his farm after his death: who will do it, how, and so forth. Life insurance comes along as a natural consequence of this planning. So, first sell the need to plan, and then the sale of life insurance will be a natural second step.

Some farms are owned as family partnerships. What's true of the normal business partnership is also true of the family partnership: death of a partner causes dissolution of the partnership. This dissolution can sometimes mean the end of the business for all practical purposes.

Here's an example of a farm family partnership. Will and Clay James are brothers and are partners in a farm operation. Will is married and has two small children; Clay is also married and has one small child. The farm is a profitable one, thanks to the hours and sweat each has poured into it. But what happens if, say, Clay dies?

The partnership dissolves. Depending on Clay's personal estate requirements, cash will be needed to pay debts and taxes. If there isn't enough cash in his estate, the creditors' eyes will turn to the prominent asset: his partnership share. Perhaps the farm will have to be sold to raise the necessary money.

Of course, Will doesn't want to give up the farm. It's *his* business, too, and the primary source of his income. If the farm goes, what happens to his income? Where will he find a new farm? Selling the farm isn't a solution so far as Will is concerned. But he may not have too much to say about the matter if the creditors of Clay press for a sale of assets.

But let's say Will continues to work the farm. If he makes profits, he has to share them with Clay's widow and child. He doesn't object to that, in view of the strong relationship that existed between the two. But what if there are losses? If this happens, Will alone is responsible for them. It doesn't seem to be fair, Will thinks. With Clay gone, he's working twice as hard, and still splitting the revenues of the farm but absorbing the losses completely.

What's the answer? As with all estate and business planning, the solution is found in advance planning instead of jerry-built remedies after death. During life, Will and Clay can enter into a partnership agreement just like other business partners in town do. The agreement will state that at the death of the first partner, the survivor will buy the deceased's interest for a fixed guaranteed price. Simple, isn't it? It's something we recommend every day to the business partners in town. Why not offer it to farmers? Backed up by life insurance, the agreement will make sure that the farmer who survives takes over the farm and is the sole owner. The deceased partner's family gets a fair price in cash. What could be better for all concerned?

The Farm Corporation

A similar approach is used with farm corporations which have problems similar to farm partnerships. When the stockholder in such a close corporation dies, the business doesn't dissolve, but the problems facing the survivors are similar to those found in the partnership.

In most close corporations, income to the stockholder comes not in the form of dividends but from wages—working at the farm business day after day. When a farm stockholder dies, his widow may receive his stock shares, but she doesn't automatically receive his income. She has a right to income only if the corporation has the money to declare a dividend and if such a dividend in fact is declared.

Let's paint a picture of Lou, Bill, and Tom, three equal shareholders in a farm corporation. Each one brings to the business his own unique abilities, skills, and talents. Each works hard at making the farm a successful business. Let's say Lou dies, and his shares pass to Doris, his widow. Doris is busy at home, raising her children and doing a hundred and one other tasks. She can't leave her home and family to work the farm. Even if she could, she would be hard-pressed to replace the contributions Lou made. It just isn't realistic or reasonable to expect her to do so. So what happens?

In the early days after Lou's death, Bill and Tom step up their efforts to compensate for Lou's loss. They get to the farm earlier in the morning and stay later at night. Their leisure time decreases tremendously. After a while, they realize that they must hire someone to fill the void left by Lou. This, of course, costs money. A point is reached where a decision must be made on money: how much longer can income be continued to Doris when she is making no contribution to the farm? At what point does generosity stop and realistic planning begin?

The stock certificates in Doris's hands can be almost meaningless paper. True, she has the right to dividends, if any are ever declared by the business. She can vote for the board of directors, but her one-third interest can easily be outvoted by the two-thirds controlled by Bill and Tom. Thus, the business interest for which Lou worked many years can mean just about nothing to his widow.

Is there a better way to handle these problems in a farm corporation?

Of course there is. Again let me make the point: the farmer in business is just like the business man or woman in town. Their problems are similar, and the solutions to these problems are similar. For Lou, Bill, and Tom, we could propose a stock purchase or stock retirement agreement to make sure the surviving shareholders succeed to complete control of the business and the deceased's heirs get the value of his interest in cash. All it takes is a written agreement prepared in advance and the necessary amounts of life insurance.

From time to time, I run across situations where no apparent buyer exists for the farm interest. The farmer's children may have gone into various professions or other businesses, and the farmer is not in partnership with anyone else. In cases like these, I look for a buyer, such as a valuable employee, who would love to take over the business when the farmer dies or retires. Again, there is the need for a written agreement prepared in advance, backed up by life insurance. The employee purchases a policy on the farmer's life, being owner and beneficiary. I sometimes recommend that the farmer help the employee with the premium payments, either in the form of increased salary or in low or interest-free loans to be repaid after the employee takes over the farm.

This type of buy-out helps the farmer in two ways:

1. He assures his spouse and heirs that should he die, there will be a buyer ready, willing, and able to purchase the farm interest, and that they will receive cash instead of a farm interest they neither want nor are able to manage.

2. The employee, knowing that the farm will be his someday, becomes an even more valuable and conscientious worker.

A Number of Other Sales

The farm market offers other opportunities for sales.

Split dollar between a farm father and son is a good approach. The father helps his son to acquire a life insurance estate by entering into a split-dollar arrangement with him. The son is covered by a substantial amount of life insurance with minimum premium outlay, and the only real cost to the father is the use of the funds advanced in the arrangement. As the son grows more affluent, he can take over ownership of the policy paying premiums completely himself, or the father (and mother), through a gift-making program, can provide the son with funds to acquire the policy.

Farm corporations can set up group insurance, pension, and profit-sharing plans. Keogh Plans or Individual Retirement Accounts (IRAs) can be a suitable purchase for some farmers. Wife insurance is an excellent approach, especially when tied with your overall estate planning approach. What happens to the farmer's estate plan if his wife dies first? What is her value when you consider loss of the marital deduction? I have one farm client who owns $5,000,000 of insurance, and his wife is covered by $2,500,000. And this is permanent life insurance, not term.

As I've noted, the farmer can be an ideal prospect. He has financial problems which can be solved by life insurance, and has the cash to buy the life insurance necessary to solve these problems. With the proper approach on your part, the proper persistence, and an honest desire to serve before selling, you can sell a good deal of life insurance to farmers, their families, and their business associates. If you're knowledgeable, not only of taxes and estate planning but of the farmer's basic problems, you can make a good impression and be of true service.

Last year, I sold $12,000,000 of insurance to farm prospects, many of whom were existing clients. That's more insurance than many agents sell to all their prospects in a year. My success is based on what I have done with farmers all the years of my career. Your success can be influenced by farmers, too, if you make an effort to learn their problems and which solutions you can offer.

My Way

Another question I'm frequently asked is—how do you find the time? Organization and simplicity are the answers. I have never been one for long, fancy, exhaustive proposals. I prefer plain, down-to-earth language, and straight, eye-to-eye presentations. I use a yellow pad and take down the assets and liabilities. Then I ask the prospect how he or she wants to meet these obligations: with their dollars or mine? Theirs cost dollars. Mine cost pennies. I show them the options available to meet these costs. They can borrow or mortgage property or they can write a check for pennies on the dollar and allow their families or businesses to keep the assets they have.

What could be simpler than that? It is clear, concise, and understandable. Together we identify a problem and solve it with the best solution there is: Life Insurance.

That kind of presentation works best when you really believe in your product. It's an advantage I have over all agents who don't have complete faith in the benefit of what they are doing for people. And it's easy to believe in life insurance because it is simply unmatched in solving certain financial problems.

17.

HOW YOUR SPOUSE CAN HELP YOU IN LIFE INSURANCE SELLING

The title of this chapter may be misleading because it isn't really a "how to" chapter at all. The thoughts I'm about to express are based on my relationship with my wife, Eunice, and since marriage is a personal relationship, they all may not apply to the life you share with your own spouse. The ideas, however, might prove to be of help, and so I offer them for your consideration.

Eunice and I have been married for 25 years. By reading earlier chapters, you may have gotten the correct impression that ours is a 24-hour-a-day partnership, and that our family, social, and business lives are imperceptibly entwined. Without her, I would not be the life insurance salesman—or person—that I am today. Do I think a spouse is important to an agent in his or her success? You bet I do, and my career is proof of this conviction.

My wife has helped me to sell millions of dollars of life insurance, and yours can help you to do so, too. Although this chapter tells of a wife's contribution to her husband's success, the points I mention can be used by anyone—husband or wife—in contributing to a life insurance agent's growth and development. After you've finished reading this chapter, why not show it to your spouse and have him or her read it. Every agent needs a life partner, and the right reinforcement from that partner literally can mean thousands and thousands of dollars of extra income each year.

Four Ways To Help

There are four main areas in which Eunice is invaluable to me:

1. Mood Management.

2. Prospecting.

3. Money Management.

4. Business Investments.

Mood Management

Selling insurance is a lonely job at times—and a negative one. Most of the people you meet say "no" in a number of ways. There are days when it seems impossible to get even one appointment, let alone a sale. Although I've been pretty successful selling life insurance, there are times when I get depressed, when I get into a slump. Eunice senses these things without my saying a word.

She gets me to articulate my fears. When you work alone, you have a tendency to bottle up your emotions and thoughts. And this isn't good. You need to talk things out, to say what is troubling you. Half of the battle is just to say what's on your mind (frequently saying it can show just how silly some of these fears can be). The other half is to have a competent, caring person who can give you feedback on these fears. By getting me to talk, Eunice helps me to defuse my worry.

She has a positive mental attitude which is infectious. She always sees the brighter side of any situation I may be concerned with and gives me the perspective I need. The proper perspective is important to the individual who sells life insurance. You're alone with your thoughts many hours of the day, and introspection can turn into a negative, damaging process.

Eunice provides insight, another invaluable asset for the person who works pretty much by himself or herself. "Have you thought about this?" she might say, following this up with a question or comment on something which I had totally missed. No, I would have to admit, I hadn't thought about that. Her knowledge of human nature is keen, and her questions and comments are perceptive. At times, her most important contribution may be to make me realize that I'm worrying about a situation that I really can't change. Realizing this, I can go on to more important things.

Positive mental attitude is an overworked phase, but it's something Eunice has in my presence at all times. Heaven knows I can be pessimistic enough at times all by myself without any outside help. I don't need reinforcement in this area, so Eunice carefully keeps her guard up in this respect. When I get into slumps, get depressed or get down, she gives me encouragement. It may be a cheerful word as I leave for my day's activities or a positive atmosphere when we chat on the phone during the day. More important, it may be her handling many home or family matters so I don't have to get involved. If you're totally immersed in an estate planning case, especially one where the prospect's insurability is tenuous at best, you don't want to hear that the roof is leaking or that a neighbor's dog tore up some newly planted sod in your garden. My mind is permitted to concentrate completely on my business and is not sidetracked by matters that I can't do anything about at the moment.

When I come home at night and the dinner dishes have been put away, we have a chance to talk and visit about what took place during the day. I marvel at the number of things Eunice has done during the day, and I get an opportunity to run through my day: what I did, what I didn't do, what I felt, and what I hoped for. Again, it's important to have someone to listen to you.

Help in Prospecting

In chapter two I noted that Eunice has been a helper in my prospecting, and let me repeat this observation. Your wife can be a great asset to you in your sales activities, especially in the prospecting end. As she travels through her day, she is constantly running into people and situations, separate from the ones you encounter. If she's conscious of life insurance needs, she can jot down names of people who might be in need of your services.

A young neighbor may be expecting a child. A friend's son may have just become engaged. A new neighbor may be starting his or her own business. On and on the list of situations goes. All that your wife has to do is to be aware of these things and then to relay them to you. Eunice has a trained ear and a great knack for hearing of farms that are being purchased, employees being promoted, and so forth.

She's also my social secretary of sorts. She knows my business schedule and thus is able to take care of the social engagements both of us will attend. Since I work a full day, I try to keep my evenings and weekends free of active life insurance selling. By visiting with friends and entertaining at home, I can unwind and relax, thanks to Eunice's scheduling.

Money Management

Another way Eunice helps me is in the management of our personal estate assets.

We have trusts set up, and Eunice is the trustee. As such, she's responsible for balancing of accounts, check writing, taking care of payments to be made on contracts of real estate purchased through the trusts, and so on. She has a feel for this type of activity, and she has done well with it.

She also handles the household finances. If you don't have your wife doing this, ask yourself why not. What's a more important way for you to spend your time—working with life insurance prospects or writing a check to pay an oil bill? Calling on a client to update an insurance program or seeing if the month's checks balance? Remember the point I brought in chapter 11—what others can do for you, you should not do for yourself.

Business Investments

Eunice has taken a very active interest in my business and in the investments we have made. I feel that agents make a mistake if they do not include their wives in things that they are doing. If an agent comes home and tells his wife nothing about what he's done during the day, how can she have any understanding of the life insurance business? If he doesn't take her along to company conventions, how can she meet and get to know his associates? How can she learn the concepts that are popular in the life insurance field today? Your wife doesn't have to be an expert, but this knowledge will give her a greater appreciation for what you're doing.

It's important for an agent to discuss his business investments with his wife so that she can understand this important part of their estate. One thing Eunice has cautioned me about—and it's sage advice—is that my investments should not take me away from my business—selling life insurance. I've seen some businesspeople get carried away by spending more time on investments than on the source of money for the investments. It's important to make outside investment with excess capital, but the tail can't wag the dog. My business is selling life insurance; all other "businesses" are incidental. This is where your spouse can do much to help you. If she's knowledgeable, if she's capable in this area, she can carry much of the responsibility for managing investments. If she doesn't have this interest, then get the type of investment with minimal management responsibilities.

Well, that's the way we do it, Eunice and I. It works for us. On one occasion, I had the opportunity to address the leading agents of the company. As I stood before them, I noted that most of them were accompanied by their wives (and Eunice was sitting in the first row). In my talk, I said the following words—they pretty well sum up the purpose of this chapter:

> *Without Eunice by my side, this beautiful and sentimental journey would be meaningless. She's been my adviser, my guide, and my consolation. She has given me the constructive*

criticism I need to keep on target and the courage to continue when my spirits flag. In fact, without her, this journey could not have begun, nor gone so well. Eunice, my sincerest thanks for all you are to me. Of all God's blessings, this one counts first.

My Way

It seems to me that most of us, if given enough time, can become exactly what we want to become. The trouble is that there is often a difference between what people hope for and what they truly want. Sometimes this difference is slight; sometimes it is as wide as a river. For example, suppose you say you want to be a CLU, member of the MDRT, or member of your company's top sales club, someone who earns well into six figures and whose life insurance program is equally substantial. You also want to be a leader in your community and church. If these are the things you really want to achieve—if this is the person you really want to be—then I believe that you are now that person or soon will be. But if these dreams are merely hopes, I believe they will remain only hopes.

18.

A PARTNER'S VIEW: DON'S WIFE LOOKS AT LIFE INSURANCE SELLING

On numerous occasions and in speeches and talks, I have heard Don comment that "an understanding wife is an integral part of the agent team." I agree with this wholeheartedly. I have always done my best to contribute to Don's endeavors and feel that we are, in fact, part of the same "team." While he is based in his office and makes frequent forays into the field, I am based at home, observing his activities, helping coordinate his schedules, and offering guidance and advice.

Compiling Lists of Prospects

As a young Nylic wife, I can remember compiling lists of prospects for Don. Orange City only has a population of 4,000, so you wouldn't think it would take very long to exhaust all the possibilities. But a careful eye and an inquiring mind can often yield new names even from a seemingly limited market. The local town newspaper as well as our church and college newspapers were all sources to be checked regularly for announcements of births, weddings, and so forth.

Though I don't do it as much anymore, I can remember jotting down the names of new members at my women's club meetings. Also, when we would go out for a social evening or for a friendly game of golf, I would run into people who are potential prospects (either people Don had seen before or new prospects). I would gladly compile these lists since any help I could give to Don would merely be improving our "team effort."

Attending Company Conventions

Over the years, I have also tried to make it a practice to attend as many company conventions as I can. I don't mean attending in the sense of simply "accompanying" Don. Instead, I mean attending the actual business sessions, the substance of the meeting. I feel it's important for an agent's wife to be as well-informed as possible concerning insurance matters. After all, how can I hope to help Don if I'm not even familiar with the terminology of his business, not to mention any new trends taking shape in the industry?

It's at these meetings that new directions in company policy are often outlined and discussed. It's to my advantage to be as well-versed as possible. I'm not saying a wife need be an expert when it comes to insurance but it is certainly to her benefit to be as familiar with as much background as she can.

Very often, Don and I will be sitting side by side during an especially important speech or sales presentation. When it's over or when we're looking back on it at some later date, we'll find that we each took away something different from the session. Sometimes a wife can glean an insight on a certain subject which a husband just can't. Maybe it's a question of the different perspective. Especially in approaching women prospects (whether they be single women, the wives of existing clients, or even widows), the wife's point of view can often be very valuable.

Of course, I understand that it's often very hard for agent's wives to take the time off to attend meetings, especially those wives with small children or those with outside jobs. However, try to find some way to attend as many meetings as possible. Looking back, I have never missed a convention, and on only three occasions have I missed any meeting in which Don was taking part.

Actually, I'm very grateful to our company over the years for including the wives. The little bit of background I gain at a session might be just all I need to handle a telephone call from a prospect or client which might come in while Don is away. And this certainly seems preferable to having to sound ignorant by telling the caller that Don will just have to call back when he returns.

It often seems to me that a wife's attending meetings with her husband can go a good way toward making a strong marriage even stronger. Providing everything can be arranged at home, of course, attendance at conventions allows couples to get away for a few days. Few husbands and wives get to spend as much time together as they'd like. Here there are none of the pressures of home. The meetings are almost always held in beautiful locations, and there is usually a wide variety of leisure activities to pursue when the business sessions are over. The husband is at the meeting because he has done well and it's nice for his wife to be there to share this moment of recognition with him.

Over the years, Don and I have made a number of close friends at these meetings, and we look forward to renewing these old friendships each year as well as the possibility of making new ones. Our children are grown now and are able to take care of themselves in my absence so there has been nothing to keep me from going along. At these meetings, we've had the opportunity to visit with people from all different parts of the country, from all different backgrounds, and this has been quite enlightening.

Following in Their Parents' Footsteps

It's also been quite encouraging to see the sons and daughters of our friends following in their parents' footsteps and becoming life insurance agents as well. This is a trend we've noticed with increasing frequency. Not only do these young people choose careers for themselves, but many then go on to become top producers as well. These last two years we've begun meeting with them at the various convention levels, and it's a real pleasure.

Our daughter, Debbie, has already chosen a career as a nurse, but if Tim, our son, should decided to follow in Don's footsteps, I wouldn't be at all unhappy. Of course, the final decision is up to Tim, but both children have certainly seen the benefits that life insurance selling has given us. They have seen the sincerity and concern with which their father goes about selling insurance, and they have seen the financial and social rewards which have come to us in return for his hard work. Most important, they know how much Don loves his work and how much pride he takes in doing it well.

If Tim should choose a career in insurance, we would certainly help him all we could. Parents have to be careful though, not to help their children too much. While we'd certainly want him to join New York Life, it might be wiser for a son to start work under someone else's tutelage, rather than come into his father's office. After all, it would be very easy for a father to say, "go do this," or "that isn't the way to do it." While some of that is healthy, it might be better for the boy to find out for himself.

A Rewarding Decision

I can't really think of another job in the Orange City area in which Don could have advanced as far as he has. We never dreamed when we started out back in 1957 that it would be this exciting or this rewarding. When I think back to that important day when we first made the decision I can remember Don saying: "Well, if I'm able to make $10,000 or $12,000 a year, that would be good." Don thought that if he went into teaching and could become superintendent of schools, his highest salary would be in the neighborhood of roughly $35,000. He kept thinking, "Now wouldn't that be great, to be able to do as well in the insurance industry." Of course, he's far exceeded that.

We've had the benefit of Don's success. He's doing something he likes, and he's still a young man. A teaching career might have been rewarding. But I don't think it would have been as exciting as all the things we've seen, the places we've been, and the really wonderful people we have met along the way. I've always felt that I am part of Don's business, and I sincerely hope the company and management will always encourage spouses. I'm very sure that if the wife is enthusiastic, her husband will receive the encouragement he needs to succeed.

My Way

Whenever a client comes into my office, whether it's for service work or to ask a question or just to say hello, my secretaries recognize that this is a sales opportunity for me. While the client is in my office for whatever reason, they will bring me the file and at that time, I'll try to cover all his or her possible needs. This to me is a sales interview. My client may not know it, but I know it.

19.

THE RACE NEVER ENDS

Let's go back to the first chapter. You'll recall that I told you that I had aimed at the presidency of my company's Top Club and that for two years, I made vice president. Close—but no cigar. In both years, I was beaten fair and square by two fellow agents who earned more in first-year commissions than I did. There weren't many tears shed for me because in the first year, I paid for $18,000,000 of life business, and in the second year, I paid for $23,000,000. Mixed emotions? Of course, I had them. I didn't reach the goal I had set, but what I did accomplish by stretching was very satisfying.

The third year (where I left you in chapter one), I did make the presidency of the Top Club. The $31,000,000 of business I paid for that year helped me to cinch it. I would be less than honest with you if I didn't say that making the presidency was just a bit more important than paying for that large amount of business—and the commissions it entailed.

Another Goal in Sight

Yes, money is important, but so is accomplishing what you set out to do. I'm proud of my company, and I respect my fellow agents. To be termed "number one" in my company is an achievement, and after three years, I had earned it. Running for the presidency of my company's Top Club is somewhat like a runner who sets his sights on winning, say, the Boston Marathon. You don't get ready for a big race in a year. It takes a great deal of practice, conditioning, experience, and—desire. Many good runners will never win a marathon. To some, that's not important. To others, it is. It calls for time, effort and, perhaps, heartbreak. It means sometimes coming in second or third. Very few people do it the first time out.

And so—I won the presidency. At this point, most stories would end, with the winner going home, wearing laurels, glowing with achievement, his or her name enscribed in the record books of time. But not so with my story. There was another goal in my company, and I couldn't resist it. This time, I set my sights on the chairmanship of the company's Top Club Advisory Board of Directors. To do this, you first must attain the presidency. And I had done so. Now a new challenge was before me.

Someone has researched the matter and told me that only one person in New York Life history had ever—in a three-year period—won the vice presidency, the presidency, and the chairmanship of the Top Club. That was Ben Feldman, the legend in his own time. Only Ben had done that, I thought, and the thought stayed with me.

By now, you know that I'm a goal setter and, contemplating that goal, I *wanted* to do it. I had run at full speed for three years, exhausting prospect sources and draining every bit of energy in my body, but I still wanted to do it.

I had momentum going. You know what momentum is. You've sold three cases this week, and it's only Tuesday evening. You've got three or four more working days this week, and you feel invincible. You can sell anyone. With this momentum, this running at top speed for three years, I reasoned, now was no time to quit.

A Championship Year

Let's throw in one more factor. Since I was president of the Top Club, I was invited to attend six company Club meetings, traveling from east to west and from north to south. Each trip took at least a week out of my work schedule—a loss of approximately 12 percent during the year. To this, add side trips, speaking engagements, vacation time, and so on.

Despite this time away from my office, I paid for 199 policies. The face amount of the business I sold was $28,000,000, and the premiums involved were $525,000. I maintained that being Top Club president would not make me a changed person, and that I would try to continue to do my job as an agent. So, I didn't rattle the cages or clang the bells. Instead, I went right back to work. I tried to keep everything as normal as possible.

Making abrupt changes in my lifestyle isn't good for me. I like to stay in the habit of things: the habit of calling on people and visiting with them about their insurance needs. Had I relaxed the habit for six or eight months, I might have found it difficult to get back in the swing of things.

I did find that being Top Club president gave me added confidence that I was able to transmit to others. There were many people who knew of my accomplishments. In my visits with them, I felt very confident to talk with them about their insurance problems. This confidence perhaps spilled over into their laps. Consequently, they were willing to reveal a lot about their businesses, their families, and their financial situations that prospects don't usually reveal.

To make a long story short, I did attain the chairmanship of the Advisory Board of Directors, with the three-step achievement—vice president, president, chairman—all taking place within three years.

The Importance of Goals

Would I have worked as hard the past four years if it hadn't been for the goals of the presidency and chairmanship? I don't think so. As I have said, I am a goal-oriented person and going after goals has brought out the best in me. I hope to become chairman of the board each year. Within my company, what other goals are left for a Top Club president?

Goals are very important for me. And goals should be important for you, too. Do you sometimes wonder why managers and companies set out goals? Think of the company and industry goals you've been challenged with:

- Million Dollar Round Table
- National Quality Award
- National Sales Achievement Award
- Chartered Life Underwriter
- Company Club or Convention Qualifications
- Club Officer (Such as Top Club President)

The list varies by company, but the primary goal areas seem to be:

- Amount of Life Insurance Sold
- Persistency of Business Sold
- Number of Policies Sold

- Amount and Depth of Professional Knowledge
- First-year Commissions (and Other Earnings)

These are the goals by which many in the industry set their standards. They're important. They help to bring out the best in you. The more insurance you sell, the better protected the public is. The more persistent the business is, the better protected your clients are. The more policies you sell, the more people you serve. The better your knowledge, the more competent your recommendations. The more you earn, the better you serve your family.

I'm a goal-seeker, and I like to work. Only if I have a goal to shoot for can I see some sense of accomplishment. If you take away all the goals, there's not much left. For example, if there weren't something like MDRT, would you stretch at the end of the year to qualify for the Round Table? If it takes $20,000 of first-year commissions to achieve a company club, would you stretch to move from $18,600 of first-year commissions to $20,000?

Yes, insurance sales people are self-motivated to do their best to accomplish what they set out for. But it's good to have help in setting goals.

Succeeding in Life Insurance

To really succeed in life insurance, I think it's important to remember certain things.

Seek important goals. Only those goals are worth working for and only those goals will bring out the best in you.

Develop a large clientele base. Case rate is so important to the life insurance agent. Unless you can build a large, solid base of clients, you may be continually looking for "the big case."

As someone who has had a few big cases in his time, I don't underestimate the value of such a case. But they can't be counted on to provide a continuing pattern of success year after year.

It may seem more difficult to succeed with large numbers of cases, but that is the surer way. More applications written mean more volume sold. The more clients you develop, the more places you have to go back to in the future to achieve your higher goals.

The more cases you write, the less a lapse will hurt you. More cases will permit you to place equal value on all clients without placing undue importance on any one person.

As I said, I hope to become chairman of my company's Advisory Board of Directors year after year. The competition is stiff, and I have some mighty strong people in the running with me. The goal is a worthy one, and I will do my best to make it.

The race for honors has been a worthwhile and happy one and that race never ends.

My Way

With a business owner, I let him know that I'm not there to sell, say, keyman insurance or pensions. I'm aware of all problems and am equipped to provide solutions for these problems. I want to find out which area he's ready to make a move in—what's his primary area of concern? Then I try to lead him into logical series of steps to the solution of these problems. I don't say, "Here's what you should do" at the start. First find his hot button.

20.

IN CLOSING

Closing is important to any life insurance agent. It's time to drive home the advantages of the presentation, to point out the benefits to the prospect. Let me use this chapter to close, too.

You've read the book, and I hope you found it interesting and valuable. I'm adding this final chapter as a suggestion for possible action on your part, to tie things together, and to help you do some of the things that I've done which are successful. Let's go over the foregoing material briefly and see what you might like to add to your operation.

Beginning at the beginning, let's look at chapter one, "The End of the Race." I think it's important for you to review the geographical market in which I work. Too many times, I've heard agents say that they'd be more successful if—if they had a better market . . . *if* their town had more people . . . *if* the people were more affluent . . . *if* the people were more insurance conscious, and so on. As I mentioned, Orange City is in the middle of America and the population of the town is 4,000. It's not New York City with millions of people, but I've made a very good living there. I mention this solely because *I think any agent can succeed in his or her market by doing the right things, by having the right objectives, and by working hard.*

In the first chapter I mentioned the importance of a high case rate, and I referred to it several times during the book. Yes, I know other agents have succeeded by writing big cases—and not too many cases. I've seen a few agents along the way who decided to be big case writers, to concentrate on wealthy prospects who had big needs for insurance. I don't know where these agents are today, and I don't know if they're selling life insurance for a living. I just happen to think that's not the way to go, especially when you're relatively new to life insurance.

In that chapter, I touched on attitude, what I try to have in mind when I sit down with a prospect. It's not to sell life insurance, *it's to solve the problem that the prospect has.* You must take pride in being a professional. It's never too early to start with this attitude. Sales are important, yes, but your professional approach to people is important and the key to such sales.

I finished that chapter with a word on momentum, of not letting up once you're moving well. I picked up this thread again throughout the book, especially when discussing case rate. It's only human to ease back a bit when things are going well, but to succeed in life insurance, *you must never let up when the momentum is going with you.*

Prospecting

In chapter two, I talked about prospecting. In reading it, you saw that I was like any other life insurance agent when I started. I was looking for the names of people who needed insurance, and I had no special secrets in finding such people. *The key to my early prospecting was (again) the development of a high case rate.* I worked hard and sold lots of people—and these people over the years were sources of more and more sales. Eighty percent of my present business comes from policyowners. *The more I wrote then, the more I write now.* That's an important point.

I mentioned that my clients grew, and I grew with them. The clients you write will grow, and it's your duty—and opportunity—to grow with them. The young sales clerk you write today may be the store manager tomorrow and the future company executive. The quality of your present prospecting influences the quality of your future sales. *The better they are today, the better you will be tomorrow.*

And don't overlook my system for qualifying prospects—the A, B, and C system, refined to AAA and AA in my drive for presidency of the Top Club. The system tells me how to budget my time, and I recommend it to you. It's important that, as you grow more experienced, you continue to experience the challenge of life insurance selling. Even after 20 years, selling life insurance should be exciting and fun. Such a prospecting system will help to make it so for you.

As I noted in chapter three on approaching, I find it important to set up a schedule of personal interviews with my clients each year. I find it important to go back—on a regular basis—to people I sell to see if the insurance job I did is still right for them. That's important for you, too. It's a golden opportunity to set up future appointments with preconditioned prospects. It's important to keep in touch with your clients. When their needs for insurance arise, you want them to think of you and to call you. They'll do that if you've done a good job at the start, and if you've kept in touch.

Interviewing

Your early life insurance training may have been an influence on the amount of talking you do in an interview. As I've noted, the weakness sales people have sometimes is *talking too much and listening too little.*

The chapter on interviewing techniques illustrates the importance of questions during the interview. *Questions force you to talk less and listen more.* Questions get the prospect to give you important information so that you may be of better service. I think questioning gives you a truly professional approach. Picture your reaction if, when you went to a physician, he or she asked for no symptoms and simply launched into a monologue about a new patent medicine or surgical technique that appeared to be just right for you. If this happened, you'd quickly excuse yourself from the physician's office in search of one who had a more professional approach. How do you think prospects react when you call and launch into a monologue about a new policy or "tax-favored" plan which is just the right thing for the prospect, about whom you seem to know very little?

I suggest that you devise a good list of questions that you can use when calling on a prospect, questions that secure the type of information you need in the type of work you do. As your knowledge and expertise increase, the list of questions will change.

When you close a case, *use that opportunity to plant seeds for the next sale* you'll make to the client, his or her family, or business. It's like the professional baseball player in a game. Waiting for the ball to be hit to him, he decides where to throw it once he catches it. If the tying run is on second base, the right fielder may decide to throw home to cut off the run. If the ball is hit to the left fielder, he may decide to throw to third base for the out.

In any event, each player knows what he'll do. He anticipates. The life insurance agent has to be prepared in the the same fashion: *if he or she closes the case, what will be the next idea to present?* If the agent isn't prepared, he or she may simply thank the client for the sale and that's it. But if the agent knows that he or she wants to present the idea of wife insurance, this is the idea the agent seeds when he or she writes the app on the husband. It's simply a matter of being prepared.

After you've sown the idea, take advantage of it by bringing it up when you deliver the policy. If the prospect isn't ready for the idea, *don't forget to jot down the date when he or she thinks he will be ready.* In this way, *you'll never have to start a repeat sale from scratch.* No more cold calls when calling on your clientele.

Rated Policies

All agents get rated policies. If the needs have been sold in solid fashion, it's easier to place a rated policy. And, as I noted, *don't you be the first person to tell the client of the problem.* Let the examining physician get that point across to the applicant. Be very positive in your presentation of the rated policy: the policy is a standard policy in his or her health classification. *Don't be defensive.* It's not your problem, it's the applicant's problem. And the need for the insurance is even greater now that the medical impairment has surfaced.

How is the persistency of your business? You'll agree that it doesn't pay to spend so much effort in writing business only to have some or much of it drop off the books after only a few premiums have been paid. *Persistency begins with the quality of the prospect with whom you work.* It depends, too, on the type of selling you do, fitting the insurance you sell to the needs of the prospect. How aware do you make the prospect of his or her need for insurance? Are you overselling, or are you interested in building a client relationship through which you'll sell more and more insurance over the years?

If a policy does lapse, *what is the procedure you've established to follow up on the lapse?* I've told you of the procedure I follow, and it works well for me. But what is *your* procedure? If you don't have one already, why not follow my four-step plan to reinstate a lapsed policy?

In chapter eight, I tell how I write from four to eight cases a week. If I leave you with no other thought from reading this book, let it be the importance of case rate. I can't say enough about it, and I hope the tips in this chapter help you to increase your case rate. I suggest that you establish a short-term goal of increasing your rate by, say, two or three cases a month. That's not much, but it's an increase which can dramatically prove to you—over the short run—the value of increased case rate.

Begin to think of your policyowner file as a gold mine of future sales. Some agents never seem to think of their policyowners as "prospects." Prospects are always names to be found elsewhere, they seem to think, but never in their own client file.

Case rate is a state of mind, a goal to be with you daily. If you concentrate on it every working day, there is no way not to increase it.

Slumps

Slumps are things to avoid, and you can do so if you observe the points I discussed in chapter nine.

• Don't be bored with the business. Find fulfillment in it.

• Don't get bogged down in details which someone else can handle for you. Remember your primary business is selling life insurance.

• Don't confuse "doing something" with "activity."

• Don't get stale. Look for an occasional change of pace from selling life insurance.

• Continue to challenge yourself with higher and more exciting goals.

• Don't let your mind get you into a slump. Don't be negative.

• Be prepared to pay the price of success.

The guidelines for a new agent in chapter 10 can be read profitably by an agent, no matter how many years of experience he or she may have. This is a lonely business. You tend to run on instinct at times. The comparison of Joe and Chuck in that chapter is a valid and valuable one. You have to be more like Chuck and less like Joe, of course, and it may be worthwhile to keep track of exactly what you do with your hours, even if it's just for one week. See how many hours—or minutes—are involved solely with trying to get people to buy life insurance from you.

If you don't already have a secretary, I recommend (again) that you hire one. If a full-time secretary's salary seems too high, hire one on a part-time basis. *But hire one.* My chapter on secretaries covers the "why" of hiring a secretary. I think, it does a pretty good job of explaining what a secretary does for me, and what I don't have to do. Your secretary can be a tremendous business asset, fitting well into the way you do business. Don't be afraid to let your secretary use her or his intelligence and talents, assuming many of the duties you would otherwise perform. And when your secretary does well and you prosper, *don't hesitate to compensate this person well—in salary and bonuses.*

Sales promotion is an ongoing procedure, taking place day in, day out. It may be the monthly newsletter I send to clients and prospects, or it may be the caps I distribute free of charge. I want people in town to think of me as their life insurance agent, and the cost of such sales promotion items is almost negligible. Find out which items you can distribute to your market and then do so.

Don't overlook the common items like guaranteed insurability options and age changes. What better way to call on people with a definite reason: they can buy insurance without having to prove they're insurable, or they can buy insurance today cheaper than they will be able to buy it ever again. These two ideas can be very exciting. Perhaps you've gotten too close to the mechanics of the business. Visualize such ideas through the eyes of a prospect.

Try to start—or join—a study group. It has many advantages, including more fulfillment in life and possibly greater earnings. You have to continue to grow, and a study group is invaluable in this regard. Be selective in choosing a group or members, and be sure each member can make a substantial contribution. In this business, you have to have worthwhile input from others.

Your Partner

If you're married, you know that your spouse can make quite a contribution to your success. Partners in a marriage bring qualities to the relationship, and this same give-and-take should carry over into the business side. Determine what talents and abilities your spouse can contribute to your success. Perhaps he or she is a good listener or is very analytical. Whatever the spouse's talents, use them.

I hope this book has helped you. It's been fun to write, to put down on paper what I've been doing for over 20 years. As I read through what I've written, I realize that anyone can do what I've done. There are no secret methods, no gadgets, no gimmicks—just hard work and intelligent approaches to the job of selling life insurance. Life insurance has given me everything I ever wanted from a career. I sincerely hope that you feel the same way, too.

My Way

Probably one of our greatest weaknesses as agents is that we talk too much and listen too little. We seldom get the buyer into the act. It's a good idea to have a series of questions ready for our prospects so that we can get them to talk about themselves, about their plans, and what they would like to accomplish. It boils down to communicating. Keep this in mind on the initial contact, when we are selling ourselves and our service, and not life insurance as such. Prospects are people, and people can be funny. What makes sense to one doesn't necessarily make sense to another. Each has his or her own way of reasoning.